OUTBOUND JOURNEYS IN PENNSYLVANIA

OUTBOUND JOURNEYS IN PENNSYLVANIA

A Guide to Natural Places
for Individual and Group Outings

MARCIA BONTA

KEYSTONE BOOKS

The Pennsylvania State University Press
University Park and London

To my parents, Harold and Leona Myers,
who taught me that Pennsylvania is God's country

Photographs by Bruce Bonta
Maps by Abby Curtis

Library of Congress Cataloging-in-Publication Data

Bonta, Marcia, 1940–
  Outbound journeys in Pennsylvania.

  (Keystone books)
  Bibliography: p.
  1. Hiking—Pennsylvania—Guide-books.
2. Pennsylvania—Description and travel—
1981–   —Guide-books. I. Title. II. Series.
GV199.42.P4B66 1987   917.48   86-43283
ISBN 0-271-00489-4
ISBN 0-271-00606-4 (pbk.)

Second printing, 1988

Copyright © 1987 The Pennsylvania State University

Printed in the United States of America

CONTENTS

ACKNOWLEDGMENTS

I am especially indebted to both my editors at *Pennsylvania Wildlife and Outdoor Digest*. Al Holliday first accepted my articles on Pennsylvania natural places back in 1983 and entitled the series "Pennsylvania Outbound Journeys for the Family," which gave me the idea for my book title. John Jackson Hubley, the present editor, has been very supportive and has given me permission to reprint the pieces that originally appeared in *Pennsylvania Wildlife and Outdoor Digest*.

I never could have written this book without the help of the staff in the Maps Section at Penn State's Pattee Library, especially Amelia Harding, who always found the topographic maps I needed.

I also drew heavily on the many fine people at the Western Pennsylvania Conservancy, particularly Charles Bier, Paulette Johnson, Bill Randour, and Paul Weigman.

Many others answered questions along the way, and some spent hours taking me around their special places. I am particularly grateful to Evelyn Anderson, Jim Avens, Al Burd, Byron Crowell, Ed Falco, Edward W. Graham, Jr., Dave Johnson, Charles E. Marshall, Janet Marvin, Don Miller, Roger Mower, Jr., Ralph Reitz, Nancy Schuler, Joyce Barnes Stone, Jean Stull, Hilary Vida, L. Arthur Watres, and Barbara Wicks.

I was usually accompanied by at least one of my three sons—Steven, David, and Mark—who always volunteered their individual perspectives.

And finally, my husband, Bruce, was my companion, my chauffeur, and my photographer. He also used his precise mind to make directions to each place as clear and accurate as possible. Together we enjoyed exploring natural Pennsylvania.

To my readers: A guidebook is only as good as the author's information sources. Although I have combed the state to find what I consider the fifty-five best natural places, I am certain there are hidden nooks I have not discovered. If you know of such a place, please write to me in care of the publisher.

SOURCES

You must have a good map of Pennsylvania to follow the directions in this book. The best map is the Official Transportation Map put out by the Pennsylvania Department of Transportation. This map clearly shows most of the state and federally owned parks, natural areas, and forests, including twenty-eight of the fifty-five places covered in *Outbound Journeys*. To get a complimentary copy, write to the Bureau of Office Services, Pennsylvania Department of Transportation, Harrisburg, PA 17120, or contact your local state legislator's office and ask to have a map sent to you.

An informational brochure (with map) highlighting thirty-seven projects of the Western Pennsylvania Conservancy, twelve of which are featured in this book, is available free for those interested in joining the Conservancy. Write to the Western Pennsylvania Conservancy, 316 Fourth Avenue, Pittsburgh, PA 15222.

Make it a habit, when visiting state parks, of stopping first at the park office to pick up the park brochure and map. You can also write or call the Office of Public Information, Department of Environmental Resources, P.O. Box 1467, Harrisburg, PA 17120 (717-787-2657), to request specific park maps. Furthermore, using the Official Transportation Map as a base, the Department of Environmental Resources issues an annual State Parks Recreational Guide and a Pennsylvania Trail Guide.

Places with visitors and/or nature centers almost always have trail maps and informational brochures, in addition to personnel willing to answer any of your questions.

The Pennsylvania Game Commission, P.O. Box 1567, Harrisburg, PA 17120, can supply maps of state game lands. The Allegheny National Forest, Box 847, Warren, PA 16365, publishes a Forest Recreation Map, which includes information on camping, picnicking, and other recreational uses.

For maps and informational brochures about state forests, write to the Department of Environmental Resources, Bureau of Forestry, 3rd and Reily Streets, Harrisburg, PA 17120. The Mt. Davis Forbes State Forest brochure, for instance, has several pages on the human and geologic history of the area as well as a map of the hiking trails.

Finally, consult the selected bibliography at the back of this book. *Pennsylvania Hiking Trails in State Parks, Game Lands and Elsewhere* is particularly useful because of its accurate, up-to-date trail maps.

INTRODUCTION

Pennsylvania is a state of outstanding natural beauty. This comes as a surprise to many outsiders visiting Pennsylvania for the first time. Such visitors usually expect to see two large cities, Pittsburgh and Philadelphia, sprawling suburbs, and rural areas dotted with coal mines.

The national media have publicized the beauties of New England, the Adirondacks, and the Great Smoky Mountains, but Pennsylvania's natural wonders are often ignored. This does not mean they are less impressive than better-known places; on the contrary, they are simply undiscovered. Yet some Pennsylvanians know better. While other Easterners flee their states for vacations and weekend jaunts, these Pennsylvanians explore their own state.

Pennsylvania has superlative state parks, state forests, and state game lands, all crisscrossed with thousands of miles of dirt roads and hiking trails. There are nature preserves, a national forest, National Natural Landmarks, a national recreation area, environmental-education centers, and several dozen officially designated Natural Areas. In such places people interested in the outdoors can find a variety of environments to explore—rivers, lakes, bogs, mountains, even a remnant of prairie. There are many interesting geologic features, private lands open to the public, and the preserved homes and property of such pioneering naturalists as John Bartram, John James Audubon, Daniel Boone, and Gifford Pinchot.

This book covers a variety of areas that should appeal to people of all ages.

Each place has been selected because of its special characteristics: an unusual profusion of wildlife, an outstanding species of flora, a unique natural phenomenon, or a locality with natural-historical significance. Most of the places are an easy drive from Pennsylvania's cities.

You need not be a long-distance hiker or in perfect physical condition. The author is a rambler rather than a hiker and is well into middle age. With this book the great majority of people can enjoy a thoughtful appreciation of Pennsylvania's natural beauties. So emerge from your cars, stretch your legs, and discover what convinces knowledgeable outdoor people that Pennsylvania is a state of magnificent natural places.

EASTERN PENNSYLVANIA

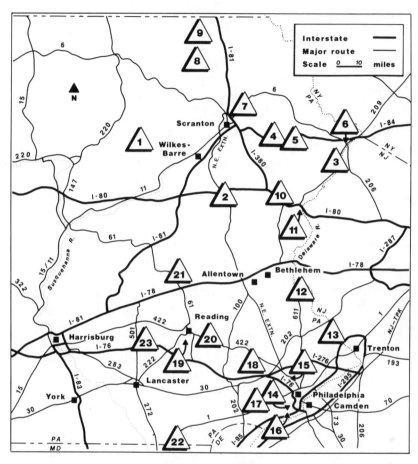

1. RICKETTS GLEN STATE PARK
2. HICKORY RUN STATE PARK
3. DINGMANS FALLS
4. THE LACAWAC SANCTUARY
5. BRUCE LAKE NATURAL AREA
6. GREY TOWERS
7. ARCHBALD (POTHOLE) STATE PARK
8. WOODBOURNE FOREST AND WILDLIFE SANCTUARY
9. SALT SPRINGS STATE PARK
10. TANNERSVILLE CRANBERRY BOG PRESERVE
11. DELAWARE WATER GAP
12. RINGING ROCKS COUNTY PARK

13. BOWMAN'S HILL STATE WILDFLOWER PRESERVE
14. JOHN BARTRAM'S GARDEN
15. ANDORRA NATURAL AREA
16. TINICUM NATIONAL ENVIRONMENTAL CENTER
17. JOHN J. TYLER ARBORETUM
18. MILL GROVE
19. NOLDE FOREST
20. DANIEL BOONE HOMESTEAD
21. HAWK MOUNTAIN SANCTUARY
22. THE NOTTINGHAM SERPENTINE BARRENS
23. MIDDLE CREEK WILDLIFE MANAGEMENT AREA

1 RICKETTS GLEN STATE PARK

Just twenty-two miles west of Wilkes-Barre is the crown jewel in Pennsylvania's state-park system. Ricketts Glen State Park, in Sullivan, Columbia, and Luzerne counties, has 13,050 acres of wild mountain land, two dammed lakes, a large tract of virgin hemlock forest, twenty miles of hiking trails, and, most spectacular of all, a stream that produces twenty-three named waterfalls as it tumbles down North Mountain.

Ricketts Glen State Park was originally part of an eighty-thousand-acre estate owned by Colonel Robert Bruce Ricketts, who led Battery F during Pickett's Charge at the Battle of Gettysburg. In the 1920s the Ricketts family sold more than half the property to the Pennsylvania Game Commission, and the remainder, including the waterfall or glen area, was approved as a national-park site in the 1930s, the closest Pennsylvania has ever come to having a national park. But World War II intervened, and the area was sold instead to the Commonwealth of Pennsylvania for a state park.

For years Ricketts Glen was a secret to all but its neighbors, and even today it seems to be primarily visited by local residents. But for the hikers and waterfall-lovers who do seek it out, the seven-mile-long Glen Trail along Kitchen Creek is the highlight of any visit.

It is best to begin the hike at the bottom of the mountain, beside Pennsylvania Highway 118, where there is a parking lot on one side and a picnic ground on the other. Next to the parking lot, Evergreen Trail leads to thirty-six-foot-high Adams Falls, a rugged tumble of water that merely whets a waterfall-lover's appetite.

Another waterfall cascades underneath the highway bridge. Across the highway Glen Trail winds upstream for more than a mile through a magnificent hemlock-beech forest. Many of the virgin hemlocks are more than five hundred years old, and a Bloomsburg University professor, back in the 1930s, found a hemlock stump with 969 rings.

In this area, which is quite level, Kitchen Creek has numerous deep pools,

Harrison Wright Falls, Ricketts Glen State Park

where brook trout can usually be spotted. It was because of the creek's brook trout that Colonel Ricketts hired Matt Hirlinger and six helpers in 1889 to construct an easy trail for fishermen. It took them four years to build it, using steps made of North Mountain's shale.

Hirlinger's original trail, with some repair by the park service, is still the only footpath that follows the creek once it leaves the flat area. Although the trail is narrow and slippery in places, it is a paradise for anyone interested in studying the mosses, lichens, and liverworts growing among the rocks. Pockets of soil also support a wide variety of fern species, and jack-in-the-pulpit is the most common wildflower.

Bird-lovers must depend on their eyes rather than their ears since the roar of creek and falls usually makes it impossible to hear any but the loudest of birds—blue jays, American crows, hairy woodpeckers—but I have also spotted red-breasted as well as white-breasted nuthatches exploring the tree trunks on the mountainside.

However, the trail, the woods, and even the birds are subordinate to the grandeur of the falls. The first falls, Murray Reynolds, is a divided, rippling, sixteen-foot-high waterfall. The next, called Sheldon Reynolds, is a wide sheet of water falling twenty-seven feet down a smooth rock face and sending a fine mist through the air. No waterfall even remotely resembles the next, and once they begin it is hard for a walker to concentrate on the path.

After three waterfalls, both the trail and the creek divide at Watersmeet. The left fork leads up through Ganoga Glen, and the right follows Glen Leigh. All the land in that section of the park is known as the Glens Natural Area, a Registered National Natural Landmark. Although it is a difficult choice, it is best to follow Ganoga Glen up the mountain since it is a gentler ascent than Glen Leigh. It also has more named waterfalls (ten) and the highest waterfall on the mountain, ninety-six-foot-high Ganoga Falls. All the waterfalls in this glen are named for Iroquois Indian tribes, including Ganoga, which means "Water on the Mountain."

Once at the top, take a short trail over to what was once Lake Rose, now dry except for a small pool in the middle of a predominantly highbush-blueberry area. After the roar of water, it is a quiet spot to eat a picnic lunch. Depending on the time of year, there is also an abundance of wildlife, such as white-throated sparrows, mallard ducks, evening grosbeaks, monarch and sulphur butterflies, and several dragonfly species.

After enjoying the serenity of Lake Rose, follow Highland Trail across the top of the mountain. The many beech trees are scarred with the claw marks of young black bears, which use them for climbing practice. Halfway along this trail connecting Ganoga Glen with Glen Leigh is a jumble of huge glacial boulders, some showing glacial scratches, and at one place a hiker must squeeze through a narrow gap between two rocks aptly named Midway Crevasse.

After a mile and a half on Highland Trail, you reach the loveliest part of the entire trail—rugged, steep Glen Leigh. Although other hikers may be seen, this part of the glen resembles a remote wilderness, hemmed in on one side by rock and on the other by surging water, and it has some of the most spectacular waterfalls in the park.

The rest of the trail, a rerun past Watersmeet, the first three waterfalls, and the hemlock forest, is anticlimactic, a time to rest your legs and regain composure for a return to civilization.

Ricketts Glen State Park is well worth several days of exploration since, in addition to Glen Trail, there are other well-marked and usually deserted trails. At the top of North Mountain is a large lake, Lake Jean, stocked with bass and equipped with a bathing beach. Camping is possible year-round since some of the park campgrounds stay open even through winter. There is also an area for group camping that will hold eighty people, an ideal place to take youth groups for a weekend.

Ricketts Glen is a good place to visit in any season. In spring the waterfalls are at their fullest, and it is possible to see more than the twenty-three named falls. One spring I counted thirty-three. During summer the glen is cool on even the hottest days, and in autumn, although the falls are at their lowest, light shines more brightly into the glen, making it ideal for taking pictures. In addition, there is a swirl of colored leaves in each pool below the falls, and the jack-in-the-pulpits are vivid with their clusters of deep red berries. Winter is certainly the quietest time to visit the glen. Few people are there, but the trails in the virgin hemlock area are usually passable. Once the glen narrows, though, it takes snowshoes and nerve to make your way up the icy trail to see the first few waterfalls in their frozen splendor.

Ricketts Glen is not just a park for hikers in good shape; there are short, easy trails for people of all ages. You can follow Evergreen Trail below Highway 118 and then walk through the virgin hemlocks as far as Waters-meet. Another possibility is to drive to the top of North Mountain on steep Pennsylvania Highway 487, park at the Lake Rose parking lot, and descend as far as Ganoga Falls. Many older people take the circular 4.5-mile trail through Ganoga Glen and Glen Leigh and then back along Highland Trail to Lake Rose. Still another alternative is to park at the Lake Jean parking lot, eat a picnic lunch beside the lake, and then walk along a short, level trail nearby.

From Wilkes-Barre: Follow Route 309 north across the new Susquehanna River bridge 8.1 miles to Dallas. At Dallas continue straight ahead on Route 415 and 118 toward Harvey's Lake. After 2.2 miles make a sharp left on Route 118 toward Lehman and Williamsport. Go sixteen miles to the lower Kitchen Creek entrance to Ricketts Glen State Park. Route 487, north, access to Lake Jean portion of the park, is 2 miles further west on Route 118. Note: Recreational vehicles and cars pulling trailers are not permitted on this very steep mountain road. For them, access to Lake Jean is as follows: Proceed 8 miles further west beyond junction of Route 487, branch right on Route 239, then continue straight ahead on Route 42 and right on Route 220 into Muncy Valley. Continue on Route 220 north to Dushore. At Dushore proceed south on Route 487 to Lake Jean. (This roundabout route is approximately 55 miles.)

2 HICKORY RUN STATE PARK

Hickory Run State Park, on the Pocono Plateau in Carbon County, is an hour's drive from the Wilkes-Barre–Scranton area. It has a number of attractions, but certainly its most renowned feature is the largest boulder field in the East, a National Natural Landmark. The surrounding woods contain, according to Erdman and Weigman's *Preliminary List of Natural Areas in Pennsylvania,* "probably the only virgin spruce forest in Pennsylvania." Other interesting stops can be made at Stony Point Forest Fire Tower, Hawk Falls, and Hickory Run Lake. A network of trails can also be explored, including a short one leading to a magnificent overlook above the Lehigh Gorge.

Immediately beyond the entrance sign at the west end of the park on Pa. 534, pull off in a parking area to the right for a short jaunt on Fire Line Trail. After walking a couple hundred yards, bear to the right. Proceed .2 mile until you reach a broad dirt road. Take the left fork and continue .3 mile back to the view of the Lehigh Gorge. You can follow along the ridge top for a short way and then retrace your steps to your car.

Continue on Pa. 534 for 2.8 miles and then turn left onto a paved park road. After .7 mile it becomes dirt. There turn right and go .5 mile until you reach Hickory Run Lake. A half-mile meandering trail circles the small dammed lake, leading the walker past teaberry, sheep laurel, sweet fern, and mountain laurel growing in the sphagnum-moss, boggy area at its east end. A small woodland on the southeast end is composed of hemlocks, white pines, and white birch.

After the respite at the lake, drive a further 1.9 miles on the dirt road until you reach the Boulder Field, where the road ends. The mile-long Stone Trail continues off the parking lot still heading east, but it is not necessary to go any further to view the field.

The Boulder Field is flat and consists primarily of red sandstones at its north end and red conglomerates with white quartz pebbles at its south, so it is extremely colorful. Geologists have determined that it is located less than one mile from where the front edge, or terminus, of the Wisconsin ice sheet had been. Underneath the twelve-foot-deep pile of boulders are the headwaters of Hickory Run. The 1,800-foot-long field is surrounded by high ridges on both its north and south sides that are composed of the same rocks as in the Boulder Field.

These ridge rocks are arranged in blocks, with weak areas called fractures. When water seeps into the fractures and freezes, the rocks break away from the ridges. During the Wisconsin Ice Age, which ended twenty thousand years ago, this area was as cold as Greenland is today near the Greenland ice

Boulder field, Hickory Run State Park

cap. The ground was permanently frozen, and in summer severe freezing and thawing caused the sand, clay, and ice, mixed in with the boulders that had broken off the ridges, to slide down the slope over the still-frozen ground beneath. For many thousands of years the boulders moved with the debris across the land, grinding slowly against each other, rounding their rough edges. Finally, when the ice sheet retreated and the weather warmed up, they came to rest in the flat valley, and the fine gravel, clay, and sand between the boulders were washed away by the meltwater.

But while the Boulder Field now seems immovable and unchanging, natural forces are still at work. Every autumn the surrounding forest of red maple, alder, hemlock, and spruce drops its load of leaves and pine needles into the cracks between the boulders, and slowly a humus has built up deep enough to support small plants and trees.

Other changes are man-made, such as the graffiti on those boulders close to the parking lot. But if you are surefooted you can pick your way across the field and soon reach an area undefiled by human markings. No matter how many people are ranging over the boulders, a brooding silence seems to hang over the field because all sounds are swallowed up by the vast, open, rocky space.

After exploring the Boulder Field, retrace your steps to the junction of the park road and Pa. 534. This time turn left and continue for 1.8 miles until you reach the path leading to the Stony Point Forest Fire Tower. Park on the right side of the road and walk across it to follow a .2-mile trail up to the tower. A climb to the top puts you above the rolling hills of the Poconos and provides a fine panorama.

The final stop should be at the trail leading to Hawk Falls. After returning to your car, continue east on Pa. 534 another 2 miles, driving beneath the Northeast Extension of the Pennsylvania Turnpike and pulling right into a parking lot for the falls. The trail is about .7 mile through the forest, and it has a rock-by-rock crossing of Hawk Run that takes a little concentration, although the water is shallow.

Watch carefully on the right for a small footpath that leads down to the falls. Huge boulders provide a backdrop for the falls, and the roar of the water is loud enough that you will not notice the high span of the Northeast Extension unless you look up.

Hickory Run State Park has much to offer in every season, although mid-June to mid-July, when the mountain laurel and rhododendron bloom, and mid-October, at the height of autumn color, are especially recommended. However, an old *Pennsylvania Park News* article called winter at the Boulder Field "a scene unparalleled . . . The peculiar outcropping of the pink-red rocks backdropped by the white of snow and greens of pines, spruce, hemlocks . . . provide a most unusual setting."

There are thirty miles of foot trails and twelve for cross-country skiing. Fishing, hunting, snowmobiling, swimming, picnicking, and camping are also allowed in season. Because there are facilities for group tenting, it is an ideal place for youth groups.

From the Wilkes-Barre–Scranton area: Take the Northeast Extension south to Exit 35. Then get on Exit 42 of Interstate 80 and head west 3 miles to Exit 41. Exit there and drive south on Pa. 534 for 1.8 miles until you reach a stop sign. Turn left. Continue on 534 east another 1.6 miles until you enter the park.

3 DINGMANS FALLS

If you are a waterfall aficionado, you will want to visit Dingmans Falls, in the Delaware Water Gap National Recreation Area, the highest waterfall in Pennsylvania. Cut into the eastern flank of the Pocono Plateau by a glacier more than eleven thousand years ago, the hundred-foot-high waterfall sweeps majestically down over Devonian rock that is 350 million years old.

Such a sight should be enough incentive to take the easy three-quarter-mile circular walk. But another waterfall, which is just as beautiful, the eighty-foot-high Silverthread Falls, is also on the trail. In addition, a wide variety of ferns grow in the hemlock forest and among the moist rocks beside the falls.

There is also a visitors center with an audiovisual program, an exhibit on the environment, and a small bookshop. A naturalist is there to answer questions and frequently leads walks to the falls. Near the parking lot in the shaded ravine are several picnic tables.

After picking up a map at the visitors center, walk past the picnic area and turn right onto the trail toward Silverthread Falls. The first bridge crosses over Dingmans Creek, which is the home of brown, rainbow, and brook trout, as well as dace, sunfish, and bluegill. Several species of salamanders, such as the northern dusky, northern red, and northern two-lined, live under rocks and logs beside or in the stream. Green, wood, and pickerel frogs are also common.

Along the trail look for such ferns as the evergreen Christmas fern (the most common fern in Pennsylvania) and the leathery-leaved, evergreen marginal woodfern. Spinulose woodferns, which are also usually evergreen, are lacy, large ferns used by florists, and they like the acidic soil produced by hemlock trees. Still another ravine fern is the showy upland lady fern, which often has wine-colored stalks if it is growing in shady places.

After a couple of minutes you will reach Silverthread Falls, a long, needlelike falls in a narrow rock fracture framed by huge trees. It is noticeably cooler as you stand on the bridge at the base of the falls, an ideal place for picture-taking.

A somewhat longer, still almost-level trail goes left over another bridge and after a short distance reaches a fork. Turn right toward the platform at the base of Dingmans Falls. There you can view the wildly rushing waterfall in its entirety. If you wish, you can climb the several series of steep, slippery steps that lead up to the top of the falls. This offshoot has more rewards for the fern enthusiast because in the wet, rocky ledges beside the falls ferns such as the maidenhair spleenwort, fragile, and long beech grow, as well as liverworts. At the top, through a thick curtain of greenery, Dingmans Falls thunders down out of sight.

Dingmans Falls

Finally, retrace your steps to the fork in the trail, and this time continue straight ahead through a magnificent grove of hemlocks, rhododendrons, and laurel shrubs, up a slight incline and back to the visitors center.

Probably the only mammal most walkers will see is the gray squirrel, but naturalists have also found masked, smoky, and short-tailed shrews in the area as well as star-nosed moles, long-tailed weasels, southern flying squirrels, and the ubiquitous white-footed mice.

The best time to visit Dingmans Falls is in late June or early July, when the rhododendrons are in bloom and the ferns are at their best, although in spring the falls, filled with the runoff from winter snows, are the most spectacular. In winter the waterfalls freeze.

Because the trail is so easy, short, and cool, it makes a nice outing for any age. I visited Dingmans Falls near the end of a warm summer day and found it almost deserted, but I was assured that crowds of visitors do find their way to the highest waterfall in Pennsylvania.

From Scranton: Follow Interstate 84 for 30 miles east to Interchange 9. Turn right onto Pa. Route 739. Go 14 miles to Route 209. Turn right into Dingmans Ferry. At sign for falls turn right. Proceed .4 mile, then bear right again. After another .2 mile, bear left, following the main road and signs for falls.

4 THE LACAWAC SANCTUARY

The Lacawac Sanctuary in southern Wayne County is owned and operated by the Lacawac Sanctuary Foundation. A National Natural Landmark because of its pristine glacial lake surrounded by ponds, swamps, marshes, bogs, meadows, and a mixed hardwood-conifer forest, the sanctuary has a wide variety of plants and wildlife from the life zones—Canadian, Carolinian, and Alleghenian—that surround it.

The only way to see most of the sanctuary is to take one of the tours conducted each Saturday from May through October by either the resident curator-naturalist or the former owner of the property, L. Arthur Watres, who, with his mother, Mrs. Reyburn Watres, founded the sanctuary in 1966. The tours begin at 10:00 A.M. sharp, are free to the public, and last two hours. The geology, as well as the natural history, of the property is discussed, and you learn that the sanctuary was covered by a glacier a thousand feet thick thirteen thousand years ago. In 1903 a coal operator from Scranton, William Connell, bought the property and built a summerhouse on its four hundred acres. He also reintroduced white-tailed deer in this part of Pennsylvania by bringing some up from Virginia and enclosing them within a four-mile deer fence he had built around his land. The herd multiplied, and some deer escaped and merged with a Pike County herd that had been imported from Michigan. Today there are too many deer at Lacawac despite a yearly hunting season, and signs of heavy browsing are evident in the woodland. The deer are also fond of the ten species of wild orchids, including the ragged fringed orchis, spotted coralroot, pink lady's slipper, pale green orchis, rose pogonia, and small woodland orchis, growing on the property.

Fifty-two-acre Lake Lacawac, the heart of the sanctuary, has been called "the southernmost unpolluted glacial lake in North America." Certainly you will not see another natural lake in the Poconos as clear as Lake Lacawac. That is because the Connells, and after them the Watreses, were careful not to allow any wastewater into the lake.

For nineteen years researchers from the Academy of Natural Sciences in Philadelphia have found this lake invaluable as a field laboratory for studying

Lake Lacawac, Lacawac Sanctuary

the effects of environmental changes caused by natural phenomena. Shaped like a half-moon, this "ice scour" lake has two distinct habitats—an organically rich bog to the west and north and sand and rock to the east and south. The latter habitat was formed by continual wave action from prevailing northwest winds and supports only a few plants, primarily cattails and golden clubs. The bog, on the other hand, is rich in plants, including round-leaved sundews, pickerelweeds, fragrant and bullhead water lilies, and pitcher plants.

Lake Lacawac, like all lakes, is "eutrophying," or aging by gradually filling in from vegetation, and is now a third smaller than when it was first dug out by a glacier. It is also only half as deep—forty feet—as it was originally. Thirty-five crustacean species and thirty species of aquatic plants, including the rare floating hearts, water shield, and arrow arum, have been identified in the lake. On the south side of the sanctuary, a series of rocky ledges dropping 250 feet to the shores of Lake Wallenpaupack support twenty-one species of ferns and numerous mosses and lichens, as well as a mature forest.

After the two-hour guided tour, you can explore the recently built Maurice Broun Self-Guided Nature Trail. Named for the first and most famous curator of Hawk Mountain Sanctuary, who served on the board of Lacawac Sanctuary, this trail runs through a field and into a young mixed hardwood forest of red and sugar maples, American beech, black birch, hemlock, and a few oaks. It also includes the magnificent Wallenpaupack Overlook. If you move quietly, it is possible to see black bears, wild turkeys, white-tailed deer, gray and red foxes, porcupines, snowshoe hares, flying squirrels, or even a bobcat since tracks of all these animals have been identified here, as the excellent trail guide, which you can pick up at the start of the trail, informs you.

In addition to the Saturday tours and the nature trail, Lacawac Sanctuary has a variety of outdoor-education programs from May through October and lovely facilities in the Connells' original summerhouse for groups wanting to spend a weekend at this remote Pocono retreat. Groups are also welcome on the Saturday tour if they call ahead (717-689-9494) or write to the Lacawac Sanctuary, R.D. 1, Box 518, Lake Ariel, PA 18436. Since, in the words of L. Arthur Watres, "Lacawac is dedicated to filling gaps in man's knowledge of his environment and to promoting an understanding of man's place in natural creation," they welcome anyone with an interest in the natural world.

From Scranton: Take Interstate 84 east to Exit 6. Follow Route 507 north .5 mile and turn left onto Ledgedale Road. Proceed to Ledgedale Bridge and turn right towards Landis Marina. One-half mile past Landis Marina, turn right onto Lacawac Road. Proceed .5 mile to parking lot, where both the Saturday tour and the nature trail begin.

5 BRUCE LAKE NATURAL AREA

Bruce Lake Natural Area in the Poconos is the place to go for a glimpse of the north woods not far from Middle Atlantic cities. Bruce Lake is a natural lake in a glaciated setting, with a bog at its south end and cliffs at its north. The understory in the woods consists not only of mountain laurel and lowbush blueberries but also of pink-blossomed sheep laurel, the common laurel of northern New England. Other species more prevalent in the northern bog forests are the shrub leatherleaf and black spruce, balsam fir, and tamarack. The floating sphagnum-moss bog at the south end of Bruce Lake is a show-place for the carnivorous pitcher plant, the bog orchid calopogon, and the large cranberry.

While there is track evidence that bobcats live in the Balsam Swamp area, more common mammals are gray foxes, white-tailed deer, gray squirrels, and eastern chipmunks. During spring and fall migrations the predominantly white oak, red maple, and chestnut oak woods are filled with warblers, vireos, and flycatchers. Belted kingfishers, osprey, and even an occasional bald eagle have been seen fishing the lake. The more common rufous-sided towhees, red-bellied, downy, and hairy woodpeckers, black-capped chickadees, brown creepers, yellow-shafted flickers, and gray catbirds are easy to observe.

Autumn, after the first hard frost, is probably the best time to visit Bruce Lake Natural Area if hordes of mosquitoes do not appeal to you. However, the array of wildflowers in April and May, the beauty of mountain laurel in June, and the bog flowers that bloom in July and August may make those times equally appealing to the dedicated botanist.

A number of old roads and trails can be explored. All are well labeled, relatively level, and closed to motor vehicles. One of the best walks starts at the Egypt Meadow Road entrance. After a half mile, the road turns left, while Panther Swamp Trail goes right. Follow Panther Swamp Trail south on the west side of Egypt Meadow Lake, an artificial, sixty-acre body of clear water. After another half mile you reach Bruce Lake Road and should turn left. This road leads to a bridge bisecting Egypt Meadow Lake. To the left can be seen the beginnings of Balsam Swamp, the largest and wildest of the swamps in the area. A short hike ending here gives one a sense of the wildness of the place.

Continue east on Bruce Lake Road toward the more remote Bruce Lake. Except for a small incline beyond the bridge, the path continues to be wide and level. Approximately eight-tenths of a mile from the bridge, extensive cliffs to the left can be seen from the road. Cave fanciers might enjoy exploring the rocks for occasional overhangs large enough to shelter a person.

Once you reach the north end of Bruce Lake, the view of a lake without a single cabin rimming its shores or a motorboat cruising its waters makes the

Bruce Lake, Bruce Lake Natural Area

three-mile walk in worth it. Several primitive campsites have been established at this picturesque spot, with a single pump to provide drinking water. While Bruce Lake Natural Area is part of the state-forest system, you must go to the Promised Land State Park office to obtain a forty-eight-hour camping permit.

The best place to picnic is on the flat rocks above the cliffs that overlook the entire forty-eight acre lake from its north end. Then, if six miles seems the limit of your hiking endurance, return the way you came.

A further two-mile circuit around Bruce Lake and its bog is well worth the extra energy expended. Less than a tenth of a mile beyond the cliffs, Bruce Lake Road leads into the single-track, yellow-blazed East Branch Bruce Lake Trail to your right. Follow this trail south for a mile until you reach a bridge graced by large royal ferns growing on the banks of the stream below it. Immediately past the bridge, bear right again on the still yellow-blazed path, now called West Branch Bruce Lake Trail. When it intersects with Bruce Lake Road, turn left and retrace your steps to Egypt Meadow Lake.

At Panther Swamp Trail an alternate route to the parking area, of about the same distance, is to go straight ahead on Bruce Lake Road. This stretch of road skirts the edge of hemlock-rimmed Panther Swamp, with its skeletal remnants of rotting trees grayly silhouetted against the black, tannic acid–stained water. However, when you reach the main road, you must hike 1.3 miles back to the Egypt Meadow parking lot.

From Scranton: Follow Interstate 84 east approximately 25 miles to Exit 7. Turn right off Exit 7 on Pa. Route 390. At .2 mile turn left into the parking lot.

6 GREY TOWERS

Grey Towers, situated on a hill overlooking the town of Milford in northeastern Pennsylvania, was once the summer home of the wealthy Pinchot family. Now it is a National Historic Landmark owned and administered by the U.S. Forest Service.

A visit to Grey Towers is a lesson in American history and culture since a guided tour through the first floor of the forty-one-room mansion emphasizes the typical life of a wealthy nineteenth-century American family. The guides also talk about the accomplishments of Gifford Pinchot, the first head of the U.S. Forest Service and later a governor of Pennsylvania, and of his parents, James and Mary, his brother, Amos, and his brilliant, accomplished wife, Cornelia.

James and Mary Pinchot of New York City had Grey Towers built in 1886 on 3,600 acres of land after James had made his fortune selling raised-tapestry wallpaper. Since the Pinchots were proud of their French ancestry, they asked their architect friend Richard Morris Hunt to design their home in the French style, but they also insisted that local building materials be used. So the exterior was constructed of Pennsylvania bluestone and fieldstone and the roof of slate from nearby Lafayette, New Jersey. They named the mansion Grey Towers for the three gray stone towers that give it the appearance of a French chateau.

In addition to Gifford, the Pinchots had a daughter, Antoinette, who married an English nobleman, and another son, Amos, who devoted his life to social reform. They raised all their children to believe in the materialistic Utilitarianism of philosopher John Stuart Mill, and both brothers agreed with him that social good meant the greatest happiness for the greatest number of people.

Gifford, following his father's lead, was appalled at the rape of our forests by a handful of unscrupulous, wealthy men. After graduating from Yale University in 1889, he attended L'Ecole Nationale Forestiere in Nancy,

Sawkill (or Pinchot) Falls, Grey Towers

France, where he was trained as America's first professional forester.

He began his career in the mountains of North Carolina as forest manager of George Vanderbilt's Biltmore estate, where he quickly convinced people of the importance of scientific forestry. Eventually he became the chief forestry adviser to and good friend of our first conservation-minded president, Theodore Roosevelt, who later said about Gifford that "among the many, many public officials who under my administration rendered literally invaluable service to the people of the United States, Gifford Pinchot on the whole, stood first." Roosevelt put his friend in charge of the Division of Forests, which rapidly became, under his energetic leadership, the Bureau of Forestry, and then, in 1905, the United States Department of Agriculture's Forest Service.

When he was forty-nine years old, Gifford married a gifted woman of thirty-three named Cornelia Bryce, whose innovative decorating ideas are reflected at Grey Towers. One of the most interesting parts of the formal tour is the view of the "Finger Bowl" pond, designed by Cornelia and made of raised stone with seating around its rim for dinner guests. Bowls of food were set in the middle of the pond, and guests would nudge them over to those who wanted them using floating glass balls. Everyone who was anyone in the business and political world of the United States dined outside under the grape arbor that shelters Cornelia's Finger Bowl.

Cornelia was a modern woman—a suffragette, politician, advocate of birth control, and opponent of child labor. She made many speeches in public and on the radio; she ran unsuccessfully for governor of Pennsylvania and the U.S. House of Representatives; and she started a school at Grey Towers to practice "enlightened" education.

For those interested in Victorian furnishings and artwork, several rooms in the mansion have been beautifully refurbished in baronial-hall style by the Forest Service. While Grey Towers itself is a remnant of a bygone era, its second and third floors are dedicated to the next century. There the U.S. Forest Service's Pinchot Institute for Conservation Studies, a think tank for the future of conservation, also manages the Grey Towers property and continues to restore both the buildings and the grounds. In addition, the National Friends of Grey Towers assists the Forest Service in restoring and maintaining the estate and in enhancing the visitors programs.

Tours of the house and grounds are offered daily through the summer from 10:00 A.M. until 4:00 P.M. Adults are asked for a one dollar donation; children are admitted free. For group tours at any time, and individual tours from fall through spring, you must call ahead (717-296-6401) or write P.O. Box 188, Milford, PA 18337.

After taking the forty-five-minute tour, pick up a copy of "The Trees of Grey Towers" in the office. Then you can follow the short, self-guided tree trail that begins across the road from the mansion and winds through the cultivated grounds, where sixty-five species of North American, European, and Asian trees, including the European copper beech (Gifford Pinchot's favorite), grow.

Finally, follow the entrance road down past a stone-walled garden and field on your right until you reach a mowed trail at the far end. This leads back into a dense hemlock and white pine forest. The half-mile trail is an easy walk that is rewarded by a view of one of the most spectacular waterfalls in Pennsylvania, Sawkill (or Pinchot) Falls. Since this area of the property is still owned by the Pinchot family, it is only through their generosity that the public may view the falls.

The beauty of the woods and grounds makes spring, summer, or fall ideal for visiting Grey Towers. It is never crowded, for an average of only 22,000 people per year tour the estate. The walk to the falls attracts far fewer people, yet it is the forest and waterfall, unmanaged by human hands, that give Grey Towers its unique beauty.

From Scranton: Follow Interstate 84 for 46 miles east to the Milford exit, U.S. Route 6. Turn right on U.S. 6 toward Milford and go 1.6 miles. As you enter Milford, look for a sharp turn on your right. (There should be a Grey Towers sign.) Drive .2 mile to the estate entrance on the left.

7 ARCHBALD STATE PARK

The only reason to visit Archbald State Park in Lackawanna County, six miles northeast of Scranton, is to see the largest known pothole in the world. Unlike the potholes that damage cars during hard winters, the Archbald Pothole was formed more than fifteen thousand years ago by glacial meltwater that scientists believe plunged down to bedrock through an approximately two-hundred-foot-deep crevasse in the glacier. The meltwater picked up enough force in its plunge to begin a whirling motion of rock fragments that were lying in a small depression on the surface of the bedrock. The continual, whirling pressure ground the rocks against each other and into the bedrock, making the rocks smaller and the hole larger and deeper.

The grinding continued over a long period, resulting in a thirty-eight-foot-deep pothole cut through sandstone, shale, and coal. In 1884 coal miners discovered the phenomenon. As they tried to extract the coal, they encountered a pile of stones from one to six pounds in weight across the face of their underground workings and extending down to within a foot of the base of the coal bed. When they finished mining the coal around the rocks, an oval pillar

Archbald Pothole, Archbald State Park

of round stones was left that went through the rock and up forty feet to the surface.

Once all the stones were removed, the pothole was evident. Near its surface a layer of gray shale, just below the thin-bedded sandstone, is smooth and polished with the typically rounded, undulating surface of a pothole.

Potholes are not uncommon, but they are usually found either beneath rapids or at the base of waterfalls in the bedrock of swiftly flowing streams. Pennsylvania trout fishermen frequently encounter them, and some have almost drowned as a result. What makes the Archbald Pothole unique is its size and undisturbed condition.

After considerable effort by civic groups and individuals, the pothole was preserved in this 150-acre state park in 1961. With an excellent view provided by a platform built above it, the Archbald Pothole is the kind of sight that elicits a "gee whiz" reaction. Certainly it is an ideal place for anyone interested in geology or for any child you want to introduce to the subject.

The park has restrooms and a few picnic tables as well as a short, unmarked trail that meanders through the woods above the pothole. During the summer the park is open from 8:00 A.M. until 9:00 P.M.; the rest of the year, from 8:00 A.M. until sunset.

From Scranton: Drive northeast on Route 6 for 6 miles beyond Interstate 81. Just beyond the Eynon Shopping Center, turn right into the park.

8 WOODBOURNE FOREST AND WILDLIFE SANCTUARY

Woodbourne Forest and Wildlife Sanctuary in Susquehanna County is the place to visit if you are a serious naturalist intent on seeing the largest tract of virgin woods in eastern Pennsylvania. Only a small portion of the 648-acre tract, owned and operated by the Nature Conservancy since 1956, is open to the public. Such limited access is in keeping with the philosophy of the Conservancy, which is dedicated to conserving our "natural diversity by protecting lands and waters supporting the best examples of all elements of our natural world." Such places are often too fragile to support large numbers of people tramping over them, but at Woodbourne a short nature trail gives visitors a taste of the sanctuary lands.

Pick up the excellent trail guide when you register at the box at the south end of the parking lot and follow the yellow markers down across open fields, into a young woods, along the edges of a sixteen-acre alder swamp, and through a portion of the virgin forest. This area contains many 200 to 400-year-old eastern hemlocks, some of them more than a hundred feet high. In 1921 a 427-year-old hemlock fell. Today the largest hemlock has a diameter

Swamp habitat, Woodbourne Forest and Wildlife Sanctuary

of 52 inches and a height of 120 feet and may well be more than 500 years old, as these trees grow very slowly. (For example, a hemlock that was aged in 1984 had 400 rings and was only two feet in diameter.) With the hemlocks grow such climax-forest hardwoods as American beech, red maple, yellow birch, sugar maple, white ash, black cherry, black birch, and red oak above an understory of hobblebush and striped and mountain maples. In addition, there is a little leatherwood, which was prized by the Indians, who used its bark for thongs and cordage.

Unfortunately, in addition to having many trees that were growing before white men settled the area, Woodbourne has an overpopulation of white-tailed deer, a more recent phenomenon. The deer are very fond of the lovely shrub hobblebush, with its heart-shaped leaves. In Pennsylvania hobblebush grows only in the colder areas, and because it is so popular with deer it is getting scarce. At Woodbourne several wire enclosures protect the hobblebush so that visitors will be able to see its showy white blossoms in the spring, its bright red berries in late summer, its mature dark blue fruit, and finally its reddish autumn leaves.

Because of its relatively high elevation (1,600 feet) in the northern part of the state, the mile-long, mile-wide sanctuary supports a great diversity of plant and animal life. In *An Ecological Inventory of Woodbourne Forest and Wildlife Sanctuary*, which curator Joyce Barnes Stone compiled over four growing seasons, she describes eleven different habitats and identifies 303 plants, 146 birds, 30 mammals, and 12 amphibians.

Along the nature trail during spring and summer, you may be lucky enough to see or hear such nesting birds as red-eyed and solitary vireos, Canada warblers, scarlet tanagers, rose-breasted grosbeaks, yellow-bellied sapsuckers, black-throated green warblers, and pileated woodpeckers. Winter wrens, wood thrushes, veeries, and ovenbirds also live in the woods.

The woodland wildflowers, specially acclimated to cool, damp woods with an acid soil, include such showy species as painted trilliums, *Clintonia borealis* (or corn lilies), and jack-in-the-pulpits, along with the more delicate sharp-lobed hepaticas, Canada mayflowers, spring beauties, wood sorrels, star-flowers, goldthread, and at least seven species of violets.

With the help of the nature trail guide, you should be able to identify twenty-two species of ferns and two of club mosses during your walk. There are actually seven species of club mosses growing in the forest; all are low, evergreen plants with small, scalelike leaves and resemble lilliputian pine trees.

The edge of the swamp also supports interesting plants—the dramatic, white wild calla in late spring and white turtlehead in midsummer. In addition, there are large clumps of royal fern and several marsh, crested, Clinton's, Boot's-shield, and cinnamon ferns growing amid the sedges.

Although thirty mammal species have been seen on the property, including such rarities as snowshoe hares, long-tailed weasels, bobcats, mink, and otters, a visitor is most likely to get a glimpse of only such common animals as red and gray squirrels, eastern chipmunks, eastern cottontails, woodchucks, and white-tailed deer.

Cope's Pond, which is open only with special permission, is nevertheless interesting to know about because it has sphagnum-covered floating islands containing two carnivorous plants—sundews and pitcher plants. In late spring more than two hundred pink lady's slippers grow beside the pond along with eleven plants of *Shortia galacifolia,* a plant on the Smithsonian Institution's Endangered Species List for South Carolina. Believed to be extinct, it was rediscovered in South Carolina in the late 1940s. Francis R. Cope, Jr., who owned the Woodbourne property at the time, somehow managed to obtain a living specimen, which he planted beside his pond. Surprisingly it has thrived in its northern refuge.

Surprises are the order of the day, though, at the Woodbourne Forest and Wildlife Sanctuary, where northern and southern bird, animal, and plant species mingle harmoniously. We can be grateful that the Cope family donated this property to the Nature Conservancy and that they and its caretakers, Joyce and Benjamin Stone, have protected it for future generations to enjoy.

Families are welcome to walk the nature trail, but groups of more than eight must arrange ahead with the caretakers (717-278-3384) for a guided nature walk. Other activities, such as spring bird walks, nature classes, and slide programs, are offered, and members of the Nature Conservancy are especially welcome. If you don't join the Conservancy, please leave a donation to help support this unique sanctuary.

From Scranton: Follow Interstate 81 north to the Clark's Summit exit. Then take U.S. Route 6 west 18.1 miles to Tunkhannock, where you turn right onto Pa. 29 north. After 14.8 miles, look for a yellow blinker light in the center of Dimock and follow 29 north for a mile until you reach the sanctuary parking lot on the right.

9 SALT SPRINGS STATE PARK

Salt Springs State Park in Susquehanna County has a short, narrow gorge with three lovely waterfalls, a small growth of virgin hemlocks, and an unusual salt spring near the mouth of the gorge. The park's 409 acres were purchased in parcels during the 1970s from the Nature Conservancy, which had bought the land from its former owner, James Wheaton.

Very little has been done to develop this quiet, pristine park. A couple of picnic tables, restrooms, and a series of short trails are all that a visitor can expect, but if you want solitude and beauty Salt Springs State Park is the place to go.

Waterfall on Fall Brook, Salt Springs State Park

After you park, follow Fall Brook through the gorge for a little more than a quarter of a mile. The creek flows over flat rock ledges reminiscent of the glens near Ithaca, New York, and the steep hillsides on either side are covered with ferns and hemlocks. When you reach the first waterfall you must turn back, but first notice the fine growth of liverwort on the wet rocks close to the falls. Foamflowers also grow along the stream.

Retrace your steps to the picnic area, and this time follow the sign that says "Path." The trail goes steeply up the hillside, where it leads through the virgin hemlocks, including one with a circumference of eleven feet. The main trail parallels Fall Brook, giving the hiker a superb view down at the three waterfalls.

The path turns sharply back to the left. After a short distance you can either follow the main trail or take a short right loop, marked by red and yellow discs on the trees, through a mixed hardwood-hemlock woods. This loop joins the main trail further along and comes out above the salt spring, which is at the base of the hill just beyond the grassy picnic area. You can definitely taste salt in the drips that ooze from the hillside.

Apparently, Indians used the spring as a source of salt long before the first white settlers arrived in the area. Shortly after the Civil War the Susquehanna Salt Works Company sank a 650-foot well. There they discovered brine, which they manufactured into approximately twenty tons of high-quality dairy salt. A local historian of the time, Emily C. Blackman, wrote that the salt "though excellent in kind has not proved remunerative in quantity."

No park brochures had been printed when we visited, but the state has plans to build more trails, erect a picnic pavilion, and restore the historical residences on the park land, so this is definitely a park to watch for future developments.

Although a ranger may be there during weekends in June, July, and August, it is best to make arrangements for group tours at least a week ahead of time by writing the Lackawanna State Park, R.D. 1, Box 251, Dalton, PA 18414, or by calling 717-945-3239. During a visit we made in mid-October, a ranger led a large group of senior citizens over the trail and explained the park's historical as well as natural significance. Because the gorge area is so cool, summer is an ideal time to visit.

From Scranton: Follow Interstate 81 north to the Clark's Summit exit. Take U.S. Route 6 west 18.1 miles to Tunkhannock, where you turn right onto Pa. 29 north. Follow Route 29 north 21 miles to the center of Montrose. Still following 29, turn right at light, then left after 1.2 miles, and continue north for about 6 miles to the town of Franklin Forks. After you have crossed a bridge, turn left onto Legislative Route 57077 and drive one mile paralleling Silver Creek until you reach the park entrance on your left.

10 TANNERSVILLE CRANBERRY BOG PRESERVE

Slogging through a bog is probably not most people's idea of a good time, yet that is the only way to appreciate the Tannersville Cranberry Bog Preserve, a National Natural Landmark in the Pocono Mountains near Stroudsburg. Owned by the Nature Conservancy and operated by the nearby Meesing Nature Center, the 418-acre tract is accessible to the public only during scheduled walks led by trained naturalists.

A bog is a wetland with evergreen trees and shrubs that is underlaid by deep peat deposits. The Tannersville Bog is between 13,350 and 16,000 years old, a remnant of an ecosystem more commonly found in the Adirondacks

Flowering pitcher plant, Tannersville Cranberry Bog Preserve

and the Canadian wilderness. Left behind in the Poconos during the last Ice Age, Tannersville Bog is the southernmost low-altitude, boreal bog in the eastern United States.

At nine hundred feet in elevation, the bog is actually below the surrounding hills, an unusual feature since most bogs are found at higher elevations. When the glaciers retreated, sphagnum moss partially decayed into peat, which slowly accumulated in the water-filled depression left in the earth by blocks of melting ice. A ridge of glacial debris, called Indian Ridge, forms the outside edge of the three concentric zones of vegetation found in Tannersville Bog.

First there is an outermost zone of deciduous trees and shrubs—alders, blueberry bushes, red maples, and sour gum trees. Gray catbirds, common yellowthroats, and red-eyed vireos are the common nesting birds here, and wildflowers like downy rattlesnake plantain, whorled loosestrife, twinflower, and arrow-leaved tearthumb can also be found.

The middle zone is a mixed hardwood-evergreen forest with a peat depth of two to fifteen feet. It is still possible to keep your feet dry in this area if you are surefooted enough to leap from one dry hummock to another. But you must also look carefully for poison sumac, which, along with white pines, rhododendron, yellow birches, and red maples, is a feature of this zone. Fern enthusiasts will find marginal-shield, sensitive, marsh, royal, and cinnamon ferns, while birdwatchers may spot veeries, hermit thrushes, and Canada, Blackburnian, magnolia, and black-throated green warblers. In this zone you may also be lucky enough to discover the small yellow lady's slipper or goldthread in bloom.

In the center of the bog, where the peat is about fifty-two feet deep, you feel as if you have been transported to the Canadian muskeg. Black spruce and northern larch (tamarack) dominate the landscape, along with highbush blueberry, sheep and bog laurels, leatherleaf, labrador tea, and bog rosemary. Cranberry plants, insect-eating pitcher plants and round-leaved sundews, wild calla, and several wild orchids—white-fringed and purple-fringed orchis, rose pogonia, grass pink, swamp pink, and frogspike—grow in the spongy floating mat of sphagnum moss. The common bird species here during the summer are Nashville, yellow, golden-winged, and chestnut-sided warblers. The Tannersville Cranberry Bog is also inhabited by the rare Muhlenberg's bog turtle.

So that visitors can see the heart of the bog without upsetting its fragile habitat, a 350-foot-long boardwalk floats on plastic drums. The Tannersville Cranberry Bog Stewardship Committee plans to extend the boardwalk as funds are obtained. Because of the boardwalk, the Meesing Nature Center is able to schedule several outings here every year. You need not be a member of the nature center or the Nature Conservancy to join in; in either case there is a small fee. Call the Meesing Nature Center at 717-992-7334 or write to them at R.D. 2, Box 2335A, Stroudsburg, PA 18360, to ask about scheduled trips.

Late June is the best time to see many of the bog plants in bloom, and I thoroughly enjoyed myself and learned a lot at a program called "Wetland to Your Knees" at that time. Ten people accompanied a guide who led us through the deepest part of the bog to see the pitcher plants in bloom. Other seasons also have their charms, and in winter, when the bog is frozen, the going is easier. Small groups, as well as individuals and families, can be accommodated on tours, but sign up early because only limited numbers of people are allowed in the bog at one time. In addition, special trips can be arranged for school classes and other large groups.

Since Tannersville Bog is open to the public only during tours, contact the Meesing Nature Center for directions.

11 DELAWARE WATER GAP

The Delaware Water Gap is part of a National Recreation Area that lies between the Kittatinny Ridge in New Jersey and the Pocono Mountain Plateau in Pennsylvania. In the nineteenth century it was famous as one of the nation's foremost natural landmarks, attracting wealthy citizens to nearby resort hotels for long summer holidays. Today it is still known as one of the best examples of a water gap in the United States.

From numerous overlooks on both sides of the river, visitors traveling by car can see the three erosion-resistant rock formations through which the Delaware River has cut over long spans of geologic time. The main rock layer visible in the gap and cliffs is quartzite, while red sandstone underlies the north end and dark gray shale the southern terminus.

To see the natural beauty of the gap close up, explore the area on foot. One of the best and easiest trails to follow is reached by parking in the Resort Point Overlook parking lot off Route 611 on the Pennsylvania side. Walk across the road and climb the stone steps to take the trail, which parallels a stream. After a short, steep ascent, bear left on a blue-blazed trail that follows along the edge of Mt. Minsi through a dense forest of hemlock and rhododendron.

If it were not for the roar of traffic from Interstate 80 on the New Jersey side, the illusion of a remote wilderness would be complete. Nevertheless, the birds do manage to make themselves heard above the mechanized clamor, and in early May the woods are filled with spring arrivals like eastern phoebes, ovenbirds, American redstarts, rose-breasted grosbeaks, rufous-sided towhees, wood thrushes, and black-throated blue warblers.

In spring the trail is bordered by a wide variety of wildflowers, from trout lilies near the base of the mountain to jack-in-the-pulpit and Solomon's seal at the first overlook. However, just before that overlook, pick up the white-blazed Appalachian Trail, which continues left along the mountain edge. From there

Stream crossing, Delaware Water Gap

until the trail crosses a small stream with a waterfall, Canada mayflowers, columbine, bluets, rue anemone, wild geraniums, mayapples, moss pink, and lyre-leaved rock cress are common sights.

At the waterfall you have walked about a mile in an easy ascent. Here the sound of water finally obliterates the traffic noise, making this an excellent place to rest. From this point it is only a short distance further along the trail before a double white blaze marks a right turn that climbs steeply up the open mountainside. Instead of taking that trail, walk straight ahead to a large rock outcropping overlooking the Delaware Water Gap—the best view of the area.

Then retrace your steps a few hundred feet until you come to a short spur that leads down toward the lower part of the same stream you forded earlier. With its thick growth of large rhododendron bushes, and a series of small but scenic waterfalls, this area is an excellent place to eat a bag lunch.

Return to the white-blazed trail and follow it back down the mountain, but just before you reach the blue-blazed spur again, take the left, white-blazed Appalachian Trail fork onto a gravel road, which, after a short descent, brings you to Lake Lenape on the left. This small lake is filled with bullfrogs and water lilies and is encircled by a faint (in places) trail that passes stands of wild ginger and mitrewort. The trail crosses a marshy area at the upper end of the lake where we saw a lesser yellowlegs that went about its business of probing for food despite our presence.

After you return to the gravel road from the lake trail, watch to your left for a trail that leads back down along the same stream you first followed when climbing the stone steps. Follow it for a few hundred feet, then cross the stream and descend the steps to the parking lot. One of thirteen trails in the National Recreation Area, this trail gives the walker a lovely overview of the water-gap environment in slightly less than three easy miles.

To get maps and information on the entire Delaware Water Gap National Recreation Area, take the Interstate 80 bridge over the river into New Jersey and stop at the Kittatinny Point Information Station just off the interstate. Groups can arrange special tours by writing to the Delaware Water Gap National Recreation Area, Bushkill, PA 18324, or by calling 717-588-6637. Camping facilities are not available in the recreation area, but private campgrounds, as well as food and lodging, are nearby. Canoeing, fishing, ice skating, cross-country skiing, snowmobiling, and ice fishing are all allowed in designated areas.

From the Allentown-Bethlehem area: Follow Interstate 78 east 8 miles to Highway 33 north. Take route 33 for 20 miles north to Route 209. Drive 4 miles on 209 toward Stroudsburg and Interstate 80. After 4.5 miles on Interstate 80 east, take Exit 53 for Delaware Water Gap and Route 611. Proceed straight ahead off the exit ramp to the center of town and turn left at the traffic light (Main Street, Route 611 south). After .6 mile pull left into the Resort Point parking lot. The trail begins across the road.

12 RINGING ROCKS COUNTY PARK

Ringing Rocks County Park in northeastern Bucks County has the largest "ringing" boulder field in the state. In addition, this seventy-acre wooded park has an abundance of wildflowers, a thirty-foot-high waterfall, a well-maintained trail with benches, and picnic facilities.

But most people visit the park with hammers in hand to make the rocks ring or, if they are especially talented, to play a tune on them, as Dr. J. J. Ott did in 1890. Ott, who was accompanied by a brass band, "played several musical selections for the Buckwampum Historical Society of Bucks County, Pennsylvania," according to John Gibbons and Steven Schlossman in an article they wrote for *Natural History* magazine called "Rock Music."

Why do about one-third of the rocks in the field ring? Scientists now seem to agree that the phenomenon is caused by high amounts of iron within the rocks. The iron, coupled with the dark, hard minerals that make up the rocks, produces sound waves when struck. The rocks that do not ring have either had the iron "rusted out" of them by moisture or are wedged so tightly by other boulders that their resonance is inhibited.

From the parking lot take the footpath at the left, walking a quarter of a mile along a level trail to the boulder field. Along the way look for such wildflowers as wild geranium, bloodroot, hepatica, rue anemone, and Canada mayflowers in the spring, Indian pipes in the summer, and white snakeroot, white wood asters, and several species of goldenrod in early September. Altogether forty-three species of wildflowers and eleven species of ferns have been identified in the park. Especially attractive are the miniature wildflower and fern gardens growing on the large boulders in the woods and displaying such species as Solomon's and false Solomon's seals, perfoliate bellworts, and rock polypody, or "rock-cap" ferns.

The birds are more easily heard than seen; ovenbirds, red-bellied woodpeckers, American goldfinches, wood thrushes, and great-crested flycatchers are all common here. The woods are mostly deciduous, with at least twenty-six tree species, although the waterfall—High Falls—is in a beautiful hemlock grove.

When you reach the boulder field you will have to climb out beyond the shade of the trees, which has helped to "rust out" the boulders at the edges, to find rocks that ring. Tap lightly with a hammer and don't chip or deface the rocks. Many boulders have already been ruined by unthinking visitors who have attacked the rocks with sledgehammers.

There are two entry paths to the boulder field, so you have plenty of opportunity to test the rocks if you are nimble. Then continue on the main path another quarter of a mile to High Falls, which drops in a thin sheet over a

Boulder field, Ringing Rocks County Park

wide, picturesque rock ledge. On a hot day the deep shade of the hemlocks and the wet rocks make this a pleasant place to visit. Finally, retrace your steps to the parking lot, having walked a little over a mile on a fairly easy trail.

Anyone interested in unusual geologic formations would enjoy Ringing Rocks, but children find it especially intriguing. There are other "ringing" boulder fields in eastern Pennsylvania, including one right outside Pottstown in Montgomery County that was a favorite place for our family to visit when I was a child. Climbing and ringing the large rocks provided irresistible entertainment for my siblings and me, but we never knew why the rocks rang or that they had taken over 175 million years to form.

From the Allentown-Bethlehem area: Follow Route 412 to Springtown. One mile east of Springtown, bear straight ahead on Route 212 (toward Riegelsville) through Durham and on to the intersection with Route 611 (4.4 miles). Turn right (south) on 611 and follow it 1.8 miles to the intersection with Route 32 at Kintnersville. Take Route 32 south 2.1 miles and turn right on Narrows Hill Road. Follow the

road up the hill .5 mile. Turn left on Ringing Rocks Road and drive .8 mile to the
entrance on the left of Ringing Rocks Park.

13 BOWMAN'S HILL STATE WILDFLOWER PRESERVE

Bowman's Hill State Wildflower Preserve, in the northern section of Washington Crossing Historic Park on the Delaware River, is the place to visit again and again to learn the many herbaceous plants that grow in Pennsylvania from late March until early October. Administered by the Pennsylvania Historical and Museum Commission in cooperation with the Bowman's Hill Wildflower Preserve Association and the Washington Crossing Park Commission, this hundred-acre preserve of woods, meadows, ponds, bogs, and barrens has approximately fifteen hundred herbaceous plants growing along its twenty-six short trails. Although most trails wind down toward Pidcock Creek, which flows through the preserve, the circular Woods' Edge Trail is wheelchair-accessible.

The preserve was established in 1934 for the conservation of Pennsylvania's native plants, and preserve personnel are still adding both habitat types and new plants. Often they are assisted by members of Philadelphia-area garden clubs, who help to plant and maintain the flowers.

Stop first at the Preserve Building. On an outside bulletin board is a list of what plants are in bloom and where they are growing on the preserve. If, for instance, you visit in mid-April and want to see celandine poppies in flower, you can consult the list and learn that they grow 250 feet from the beginning of Marshmarigold Trail as well as on Fern Trail. There are also guide lists to the wildflowers in bloom that you can pick up and take along. With these lists, a wildflower field guide, and a few questions to the friendly employees working on the grounds, you should be able to identify any wildflower you see.

Inside the building is a gift shop where you can purchase a map of the preserve for twenty-five cents, a worthwhile investment if you plan to walk the trails without a guide. Special displays, including a bird observation area and the attractive Platt Collection of both foreign and domestic stuffed birds, bird nests, and bird eggs arranged according to habitat, are also housed in the Preserve Building, which is open from 9:00 A.M. until 5:00 P.M. daily and from noon until 5:00 P.M. on Sundays.

On the grounds around the Preserve Building the wildflowers are labeled, so it is best to study whatever is in bloom there before taking the trails. Then

The Pond, Bowman's Hill State Wildflower Preserve

you may want to walk to the dam on Pidcock Creek, which can be reached by following Bucks County Trail; the sphagnum bog, featuring the swamp hyacinth and leatherleaf in bloom in mid-April and the carnivorous pitcher plant in mid-May; or the pond, with its trout lilies, jack-in-the-pulpit, royal ferns, and false hellebore.

Certain rare-to-Pennsylvania wildflowers, such as the blazing star and the blue-eyed Mary, both of which are common midwestern species, in addition to old favorites—pink and yellow lady's slippers, shooting stars, gaywings, butterfly weed, and Indian pipes—can be found in the right season. Even if you think you know most of Pennsylvania's wildflowers you will find a few you have never heard of, including the double bloodroot (the "doubling" of the white blossom occurs sometimes in nature) and the Canby's mountain lover (found only in rocky, well-drained upland woods).

Wildflowers are not the only plants featured here. The Wherry Fern Trail, named for Philadelphia botanist Edgar Wherry, who was instrumental in developing the preserve, highlights the preserve's interest in wild ferns. Penn's Woods, Pennsylvania's first reforestation program, has nine acres of tended woodlands with hundreds of Pennsylvania's native trees and shrubs.

Medicinal plants are another specialty, and along the Medicinal Trail you will see ginseng, puttyroot, goldenseal, and wild sarsaparilla in late spring. However, the lovely snow trillium, the delicate Carolina spring beauty, and the tiny harbinger-of-spring all bloom earlier, in late March and early April.

There is even interest in promoting native grasses as ornamentals, and chief propagator Ralph Reitz has been planting such grasses as prairie dropseed and little bluestem.

Birds, too, find the preserve an agreeable habitat. In spring the woods reverberate with bird song, notably that of Carolina wrens, wood thrushes, red-eyed vireos, tufted titmice, and American redstarts.

If you are feeling especially energetic, you can also walk the foot-traffic-only paved road that leads through the preserve, past Azaleas at the Bridge, and then up to Bowman's Hill Tower, with its sweeping view of the Delaware River.

It is easy to spend an entire day at the preserve, so bring along a lunch to enjoy at the picnic area near the highway entrance. The preserve is also an ideal place to visit with a group of wildflower enthusiasts, and guided tours for groups are available by calling in advance (215-862-2924).

From Philadelphia: Follow Interstate 95 north 29 miles from the center-city area. Get off at the last exit in Pennsylvania (Morrisville, Yardley, Washington Crossing). Turn left on Legislative Route 09151. Drive 5 miles through the village of Taylorsville to the intersection with Pa. Route 32. After 2.3 miles on 32, turn left into Bowman's State Wildflower Preserve. (Ignore entrance to Bowman's Hill Tower .5 mile before Wildflower Preserve.)

14 JOHN BARTRAM'S GARDEN

John Bartram's Garden in southwestern Philadelphia is a place urban dwellers can visit for a taste of the outdoors. Located on the west bank of the Schuylkill River, the twenty-seven-acre park includes America's oldest surviving botanical garden and the beautifully renovated home and outbuildings of John Bartram, the Quaker naturalist.

A close friend of Benjamin Franklin, Bartram was a self-taught botanist who explored the headwaters of the Schuylkill and Delaware rivers and roamed north as far as Lake Ontario, west to Pittsburgh and the Ohio River, and south into Florida, Georgia, and South Carolina in search of plants for his garden and for his powerful patrons in England, who paid him for the American specimens he sent them. In fact, he has been credited with introducing more than two hundred American plants to the gardens of Europe, including the mountain laurel, rhododendron, cucumber magnolia, hackberry, and pawpaw.

All this collecting was done in his spare time because Bartram was also a prosperous farmer who made an excellent living that supported a wife and nine children. In 1729 he bought the old Swedish farmhouse on the Schuylkill that he later expanded and redesigned as his family and his collecting business grew. In his five-acre garden he experimented with the cross-fertilization of plants. In addition, he used the garden as a repository for the plants he collected.

Today visitors can wander through the garden and see offspring of the many trees, shrubs, and flowers Bartram planted. The trees are labeled, so you can identify such rarities as Bartram's oak and the Franklinia tree. Bartram's oak, *Quercus heterophylla*, is actually one tree Bartram did not collect; he found this naturally occurring hybrid of the red and willow oaks growing on his farm. The Franklinia, named for his friend Ben Franklin, was certainly his most unusual discovery. Traveling with his son William, who later became a famous naturalist, artist, and writer, John Bartram found the Franklinia growing in one small area along the Altamaha River in Georgia in 1765. On a later trip William brought back seeds or cuttings of the tree and planted them in the garden, thus preserving the tree for future generations (by 1803 the Franklinia had died out in the wild).

Admission to the garden and surrounding park area, complete with a picnic pavilion, is free, but there is an admission charge to the seventeenth-century farmhouse. Open for tours Tuesday through Friday from 10:00 A.M. until 4:00 P.M. November through April, and on weekends as well May through October, it is the ideal place to begin your exploration of Bartram's Garden. Antique buffs will enjoy the period furnishings, some of which have been

Bartram home, John Bartram's Garden

returned to the house by Bartram descendants. Nature enthusiasts will be fascinated by the contents of Bartram's study—a potpourri of old botanical books, bird nests, seed pods, and feathers. People interested in American history will be delighted to learn that Washington, Jefferson, and Franklin frequently visited the Bartrams. For anyone wanting to learn more about the Bartrams and their garden, the gift shop, originally a plant room built by John Bartram's granddaughter, Ann Carr, in 1820, has a number of inexpensive booklets that are well written and informative.

Once you have gained some understanding of the man and his home, it is time to explore his garden. Turn left as you leave the doorway and walk across the driveway and onto the lawn to see the Bartram oak. Then examine the outbuildings—the seed house in which Bartram packaged shipments of seeds and plants, and the barn, which his son John Bartram, Jr., who inherited the home, built in 1775.

Two walks, each 150 yards long, lead down to the riverbank. Beside the paths are many labeled trees and shrubs, including the Franklinia, mountain laurel, cucumber magnolia, hackberry, and Fraser magnolia. Near the river are the remains of a cider press and mill used by Bartram.

The factories and refineries lining the riverbank seem inimical to wildlife, but the garden's full-time naturalist, Peter Kurtz, has made several discoveries here. Along the river's edge grows a stand of seaside goldenrod, a common species at the seashore but listed as a species of special concern by the Pennsylvania Rare Plant Committee. Birds, too, find the river environment congenial, and during the shorebird migration one August Kurtz identified greater and lesser yellowlegs, spotted and pectoral sandpipers, semipalmated plover, killdeer, and black-crowned night herons in the marshy areas.

Other birds prefer the garden. A shagbark hickory is riddled with yellow-bellied sapsucker holes, and in May and September warblers such as the Tennessee, black-throated blue, and Cape May make foraging stops during migration. Song sparrows, yellow-shafted flickers, northern cardinals, house finches, black-capped chickadees, American robins, and blue jays are more permanent residents.

Something is going on at Bartram's Garden all year long. In the winter you can enjoy tea or lunch beside a roaring kitchen fire or in the sunroom after a tour of the house. On the second weekend in December a greens sale is held. Early spring finds staff members tapping sugar maples on the property and making maple syrup. The garden is at its best in late spring and early summer, but the camellia-like blooms of the Franklinia do not appear until August.

If you call ahead (215-729-5281), you can arrange to have a box lunch provided for you on the lawn of the common garden. Or bring your own lunch and reserve the picnic pavilion. Bartram's Garden is especially geared for group tours and offers several educational programs for schoolchildren, including a botany program and such colonial crafts as making candles, churning butter, drying herbs, and designing cornhusk dolls. Box lunches, tea, and tours or special programs for groups must be arranged by telephone ahead of time.

From Philadelphia: Exit off the Expressway (I-76 east) at University Avenue. Take the first left at the end of the exit and cross the 34th Street Bridge. Proceed to the next traffic signal and turn right onto Gray's Ferry Avenue. Continue on Gray's Ferry Avenue over the bridge; then turn left at the first light onto Paschall Street. Go to 49th Street and turn left at the light. Follow the trolley tracks over the railroad bridge and bear right when the trolley tracks do; this will put you on Gray's Avenue. Proceed on Gray's Avenue following the trolley tracks to where the road forks and take the left fork onto Lindbergh Boulevard. Look for 54th Street on your right. Just after passing 54th Street, cross over the railroad bridge and make a sharp left onto Bartram Lane, a long drive leading up to the historic house.

15 ANDORRA NATURAL AREA

The Andorra Natural Area is in the northwestern corner of Philadelphia's Fairmount Park and is part of the old Andorra Nursery, once the largest nursery on the East Coast. Located in the Wissahickon Valley, which is a National Natural Landmark, this mile-wide, half-mile-long wooded plot is crisscrossed with trails through a variety of interesting habitats. In addition, many nature-related programs for people of all ages are offered free throughout the year.

Despite the proximity of the heavily used Forbidden Drive—an old carriage road closed off to motorists and swarming with bicyclists, joggers, horseback riders, and fast walkers—the Andorra Natural Area itself is almost deserted except for its abundant wildlife.

After parking in the lot off Northwestern Avenue, follow the signs to Tree House Visitor Center, where you can pick up an accurate, well-drawn trail map that enables you to explore the area on your own. From there take the road called Old Northwestern Avenue down to Forbidden Drive and turn right. The drive parallels scenic Wissahickon Creek, which has water pure enough to support a stocked trout population. Handsome old American beech and tulip trees line the creek bank, while in spring Solomon's seal, skunk cabbage, mayapples, wild ginger, spring beauties, and smooth yellow violets carpet the ground.

Just before you reach Bell's Mill Road, look for Bell's Mill Trail, which leads back into the Andorra Natural Area. Pass the first right turn on that trail and instead turn right on Harper Trail, which climbs up through the woods past sensitive fern, false Solomon's seal, and numerous sweet gum trees.

Take another right on Wood Thrush Trail and still another onto Central Loop, which ends at Cucumber Meadow, aptly named for its 250-year-old cucumber tree. A blind here allows you to observe deer visiting a salt block.

Make a short right and then a left onto Ginger Trail. Notice the many pieces of mica in the stones on the ground. Greek valerian, wood anemone, and hundreds of wild ginger plants bloom along this trail in early May. Northern cardinals, American redstarts, red-bellied woodpeckers, and scarlet tanagers were just a few of the birds we heard as we walked quietly along—so quietly, in fact, that we startled a perching Cooper's hawk and came very close to two deer seemingly unperturbed by our presence.

Many of the largest trees at Andorra are labeled with an estimate of their ages. Just before you reach Tulip Meadow you will see huge paper birch trees, the oldest of which is over ninety.

From the meadow take the Azalea Loop left and then right past enormous American beech trees and a three-hundred-year-old white oak. In this area lesser celandine blankets the ground with yellow blossoms in May, and a bird

Beech Row Trail, Andorra Natural Area

blind and bird feeder are set up during winter.

When you reach the visitors center, turn left and then right back toward the parking lot and pick up Nursery Trail on the left. Because the Andorra Natural Area was once a nursery, with 232 species and 108 varieties of deciduous trees, evergreens, and shrubs, you can still see several exotics, including Japanese cryptomeria and maples, which are labeled. Take a right on Beech Row Trail and circle an area dominated by more enormous American beech trees until it joins Honeysuckle Road. This portion of the property is more open than the rest of Andorra. If you turn right and follow the road a short distance, you will see blackberry fields growing up into saplings that support American goldfinches and ring-necked pheasants as well as the ubiquitous blue jays, American robins, and American crows.

Retrace your steps to an unmarked trail (on the map) to the right that leads to the Far Meadow and then joins Swamp Trail. From there continue on Big Tree Trail, probably Andorra's most spectacular trail because of its giant scarlet, black, and white oaks. Both red-eyed vireos and wood thrushes nest in this area.

Finally, turn left onto a spur of Harper Trail, right on Honeysuckle Road, and left on the L. M. C. Smith Trail to see "The Great Beech," as it is designated on the map. It is exactly as billed, a magnificent conclusion to a day spent within the Philadelphia city limits exploring a world most people would never associate with urban living.

From center-city Philadelphia: Follow the Schuylkill Expressway to the exit at Roosevelt Avenue (U.S. 1 north). Then take Ridge Avenue west 5.6 miles. Turn right on Northwestern Avenue, a narrow but paved alley that is easy to miss. (Watch for a Renault AMC Jeep dealership on the right and a Friendly Restaurant at the corner.) Follow Northwestern Avenue .6 mile and turn right into the Andorra Natural Area parking lot.

16 TINICUM NATIONAL ENVIRONMENTAL CENTER

Tinicum National Environmental Center in Philadelphia and Delaware counties, less than a mile west of the Philadelphia International Airport, was established in 1972 to protect the last 205 acres of freshwater tidal marsh in Pennsylvania. Operated by the U.S. Fish and Wildlife Service, it is surrounded by landfills, oil tanks, highways, and houses. Its 1,200 acres of freshwater marsh include fine trails and a 145-acre impoundment that is heavily used by migrating and breeding waterfowl.

Geese and jets, nature and humanity, coexisting in a crowded environment is what Tinicum is all about. With limited government funding, Tinicum manages to host forty thousand visitors a year. You can take nature walks led by local volunteers with expertise in such subjects as the birds, butterflies, and

Marsh, Tinicum National Environmental Center

plants of Tinicum, canoe along Darby Creek, bicycle or walk on the wide gravel trails, or fish in the impoundment.

The visitors center, open from 8:00 A.M. until 4:30 P.M. 365 days a year, is the place to begin. There you can see a small display about the area and pick up trail maps and bird lists. The birds of Tinicum are impressive—75 of the 288 species that have been identified here have nested at Tinicum. Both bald eagles and peregrine falcons have been seen during some falls and winters, and "accidental" sightings of birds that have strayed from their normal range over the last thirty-two years include the black rail, common moorhen, sandhill crane, black-necked stilt, American avocet, spotted redshank, scissor-tailed flycatcher, and both Brewer's and yellow-headed blackbirds.

From the visitors center take Dike Road and follow the Boardwalk Loop to the fourth stop. Then cross the impoundment on the boardwalk to the sixth stop. Retrace your steps across the boardwalk and turn left along the three-mile, circular Impoundment Trail, a good, flat trail that eventually passes through all the major habitats of Tinicum—tidal marsh, impoundment, and woods. Handicapped people may drive through the area, but otherwise you will see only joggers, bicyclists, hikers, and fishermen.

At first, as you walk along, you will probably notice the noise from nearby traffic and jets, but bird songs, insect trills, and frog calls will soon divert your attention. Ring-billed, herring, and often even black-backed gulls fly over the water and pose on the boardwalk, giving the place a seaside air, while Canada geese frequently take off from hidden coves, rivaling the jets lifting off from the airport runway. Watch the backwaters for other common marsh birds, like great blue, green-backed, and black-crowned night herons and great and snowy egrets. Tinicum also has nesting least bitterns, an endangered species in Pennsylvania. Mallards are everywhere, along with blue jays; American and fish crows; Carolina, house, and long-billed marsh wrens; American robins; northern mockingbirds; gray catbirds; northern cardinals; American goldfinches; and swamp and song sparrows.

Along the trail are benches and even a covered observation platform where you can rest and watch the carp jumping. A short side trail to your right about a mile from the visitors center leads to an excellent observation blind, a good place to photograph such waterfowl as black ducks, green-winged teal, and common pintails, or, if you are lucky, to spot a muskrat, weasel, raccoon, or opossum, all common mammals at Tinicum. Both painted and snapping turtles are also frequently seen there; in fact, the latter were so numerous in 1983 that turtle-trappers were called in to pull out 1,500 snappers in order to protect the duckling population.

In summer you will see green patches of wild rice, but the predominant and highly invasive grass at Tinicum is phragmite, or common reed—lovely to look at but without nutritional value for the animals. Purple loosestrife and primrose willow grow in the impoundment all summer, while marshmallow, both white and pink, blooms in August and September. Special walks sponsored from spring through fall emphasize the variety of plant life at Tinicum. Butterflies also abound in the area, beginning with the emergence of mourning cloaks in mid-March.

After you leave the bird blind and continue along Impoundment Trail, you will see on your right several small ponds, crowded with courting wood frogs in March. This is also an ideal place to spot muskrats swimming, eating, or, in October, constructing their cattail-reed shelters.

The trail continues for a short distance beyond the impoundment before turning left. In this area shrubs and wet woods replace the tidal marsh of the earlier part of the trail. Shortly after skirting the impoundment on your left, take a left and keep bearing left until you reach a right turn. Follow this path until you come to the visitors center sign, which directs you straight ahead. However, if you feel a little adventurous, turn left instead onto a series of trails that wind through the marsh beside the impoundment. Fishermen like this area since yellow perch, blue-backed herring, and golden shiners, as well as carp, are common. It is impossible to get lost as long as you keep the impoundment to your left. Eventually you reach the boardwalk; from there you continue through both a lowland transitional forest—thickets interspersed with saplings—and, along the left path of a fork in the trail, the lowland forest. A short right at Dike Road leads you back to the visitors center.

The best times to visit Tinicum are October through mid-November and in April and May, when the biting-insect population is low and the migratory-bird population high. For solitude, weekdays are best, but the volunteer-led nature walks begin on March weekends and continue through spring, summer, and fall. It is best to call (215-365-3118) to find out what is being offered.

I discovered a weekday in mid-March to be an ideal time to visit. Some of the wintering waterfowl were still there, but migration was already in full swing. I saw several muskrats close up and numerous common mergansers, common pintails, black ducks, and green-winged teal. Although the trees and shrubs were still bare, the deep purple-red of red-osier dogwood branches lent color to the scene.

The three objectives at Tinicum are to maintain habitat, to provide environmental education, and to encourage wildlife-oriented recreation in an inner-city area. Although it does not have all the facilities, trails, and programs that had initially been planned for it, Tinicum is still a fascinating place for the self-motivated naturalist to explore and, because of its location, one of the most unusual wildlife refuges in the United States.

From Philadelphia: Follow Interstate 95 south over Girard Bridge, which spans the Schuylkill River. This highway ends in an exit; follow it until you see a Marriott Motel on your left. Bear right on Island Avenue and proceed to the next left onto Bartram Avenue. Turn on the next right on 84th Street. Go through to the second signal, at Lindbergh Boulevard, and turn left. Look for a sign for Tinicum on the right off Lindbergh. Turn there and proceed to the visitors center.

17 JOHN J. TYLER ARBORETUM

Arboretums celebrate trees, and the John J. Tyler Arboretum in Delaware County near Media is justly famous for its large variety of woody plants, both native and exotic. Twenty miles of trails snake through the seven-hundred-acre property over terrain that varies from deep woods to open fields. There is even a very restricted natural habitat—a serpentine barren—found in only three Pennsylvania counties and one in Maryland.

Sequoia tree, John J. Tyler Arboretum

The arboretum is the legacy of two bachelor Quaker brothers—Minshall and Jacob Painter—who planted almost a thousand species and varieties of shrubs and trees on their three-hundred-acre family estate from 1849 until 1876. Both brothers were interested in botany and meteorology and coedited a variety of pamphlets on such esoteric subjects as a phonetic alphabet and a numerical system based on sixteen.

They left their home and grounds to a nephew, John J. Tyler, who extended the acreage. Together with his wife he also created an endowment to administer the legacy as an arboretum after their deaths. In 1945 it became a public arboretum, and today it gets its funding in thirds—a third from the Tyler Trust, a third from private donations and memberships, and the rest from an ambitious and extensive education program aimed at all ages.

For a fee of three dollars per adult (one dollar per child) you can spend from 8:00 A.M. until dusk exploring the arboretum grounds and small gardens, although if you want to picnic you must go to nearby Ridley Creek State Park. The arboretum describes itself as "a place for growing and exhibiting plants and for the quiet study and enjoyment of the natural life," so radios, vehicles, horseback riding, hunting, and unleashed dogs are forbidden here, as is the collecting of plants, animals, and minerals.

After parking in the lot behind the barn, visit the excellent education center, which includes a gift shop specializing in nature items and books and several interesting exhibits. You can also pick up a trail map and a variety of brochures about the arboretum and its educational programs.

Then step outside and explore the immediate grounds, the so-called Old Arboretum, before taking some of the more extensive trails. Several of the original trees planted by the Painter brothers grow close to the education center and the stately home (called Lachford Hall) built in 1738. As you wander over the lawn you will see a cedar of Lebanon from Syria; a ginkgo tree, whose fossil record goes back more than 200 million years; a yellow buckeye, which is a native of the eastern United States; a Yulan magnolia from the moist woodlands of central China; and an Oriental spruce that stands more than a hundred feet tall, the champion of its species in the Philadelphia area. Also take time to step into the small Bird-Habitat Garden outside the education center and the Fragrant Garden, built for sight-impaired people to appreciate. The first garden of its kind in the country, it is maintained by the Philadelphia Chapter of the Herb Society of America.

To explore a stream environment, take a short portion of the Wilderness Trail to the left of the arboretum grounds until it runs into Rocky Run Trail. Follow this loop trail as it parallels the stream and then climbs a small rise, leading you back to Wilderness Trail. If it is early spring, wood frogs will be making a din with courting noises that sound like quacking ducks; skunk cabbage will be emerging from the muck beside the stream; and purple grackles will be turning over leaves in the water. Observable at any time of the year are deer tracks. In fact, in the rhododendron display area, the deer are so abundant that a definite browse line can be seen on every bush—not a good sign for those who love both rhododendron and deer. Obviously there are too many deer for the land to support.

The open-field area is the place to see bluebirds, since forty-five to fifty pairs stay all year long in what is called the Pinetum area. The arboretum's bluebird-box project, one of the first in the state, has been enormously successful in attracting and holding the birds, so much so that the area has reached the saturation point in bluebird numbers.

Along the road at the edge of the field stands the grandest tree in the arboretum, a giant sequoia planted in 1859, one of the oldest of cultivated specimens. After admiring this enormous native of the Sierra Nevada, cross the road and walk downhill for about three hundred feet until you reach Pink Hill Trail on your right. This is definitely the most interesting trail on the arboretum grounds for naturalists, especially in late April, when the moss pink (*Phlox subulata*) makes a splendid show where it grows in the shallow soil derived from the underlying serpentine. This mineral, which gives the rocks along the trail an almost eerie greenish cast, contains toxic amounts of magnesium, nickel, and chromium and inadequate amounts of the calcium, potassium, and phosphorus that most plants need. As a result, the plants that have adapted to the presence of serpentine are both sparse and different from those growing in the surrounding habitat. Pink Hill also supports a wood-lily colony later in the spring.

When Pink Hill Trail reaches an abandoned farm, turn left onto Wilderness Trail, which takes you back to the road. Continue across the road on the same trail and return to the Old Arboretum and the parking lot.

Since the arboretum staff offers such excellent programs for all ages and interests, this is a wonderful place to take almost any group. The best time to visit is when the moss pink is in bloom in April. At that time the contrast of pink blossoms and green serpentine in the soil provides a graphic illustration of the unique character of a serpentine barren.

From Philadelphia: Take the Schuylkill Expressway to U.S. 1, City Avenue exit. Follow Route 1 south 13.8 miles. Turn right on Pa. Route 352. Proceed to the town of Lima (about a mile). Turn right onto Barren Road. Drive less than a mile to Painter Road. Turn left at sign for John J. Tyler Arboretum. Proceed .5 mile to the arboretum parking lot on the right.

18   MILL GROVE

Mill Grove, the first home in America of artist-ornithologist John James Audubon, was, his granddaughter Maria wrote, "a home he always loved and never spoke of without deep feeling." Located along the Upper Perkiomen Creek in Montgomery County, Mill Grove still retains an aura of bygone days on its 130 bucolic acres, despite being surrounded by the homes of a burgeoning suburban population.

It was, as Audubon put it, the place where he began his "simple and agreeable studies" of birds, learning to draw them from nature by shooting and then immediately mounting them on blocks of wood with the help of wires that held them up in lifelike positions. He also did the first bird-banding in

Mill Grove

North America when he tied silver threads around the legs of eastern phoebes he was studying.

Audubon lived in Mill Grove, which his father had purchased as an investment in 1784, less than three years—from 1804 until 1807. Eventually it passed into the hands of a respected Philadelphia Quaker family, the Wetherills, who greatly admired Audubon. They kept the home in immaculate condition for more than 150 years; then, in 1951, they sold it to Montgomery County as a historic site.

Mill Grove is a treasure house for anyone with an interest in Audubon's wildlife paintings. Almost every room of the old Pennsylvania fieldstone farmhouse displays his framed paintings. There is a sideboard in one room and a sofa in another that belonged to the Audubons when they lived in New York, and two bedrooms are furnished with period antiques, but by and large it is the paintings that keep visitors coming to this sanctuary.

After driving in through the gates, continue along the sweeping driveway lined with maple trees and leave your car in the parking lot. Then walk up the road past the barn on your left and listen to the bird song. If it is winter the bird feeder will be busy with northern cardinals, tufted titmice, black-capped chickadees, white-breasted nuthatches, and red-bellied woodpeckers; in early spring the eastern phoebes will be giving their monotonous, rasping "fee-bee" calls; and in summer you may see the chimney swifts that nest in the large chimney catching insects from the air overhead. At least 175 species of birds have been identified on the grounds of Mill Grove since 1951. When you enter through the farmhouse's low entry door, go left into the office and pick up a brochure about Mill Grove as well as a list of the birds found there.

Most likely, director-curator Edward W. Graham, Jr., will be sitting at his desk fielding phone calls or leading groups through the museum. With his infectious enthusiasm for Audubon's work, he can tell you a great deal about both the man and his paintings. He is an active birder, and because his home is on the grounds of the estate, he is able to keep up to date on the wildlife that still finds Mill Grove attractive. Graham is aware, for instance, of the great horned owl's nest on the property, of the Canada geese that breed on the small islands down in the Perkiomen, and of the recent nestings of rose-breasted grosbeaks and wood ducks.

The house was built in 1762, and it has the deep windowsills and bare wooden floors of the period. In the office a large portrait of Audubon is flanked by smaller portraits of his two sons, Victor and John W. Audubon. The wainscoted entrance hall is attractively decorated with a mural of Audubon's life painted by Philadelphia artist George W. Harding shortly after Montgomery County purchased the home.

The room beyond the office is dominated by Audubon's oil portrait called "The Eagle and the Lamb," painted in 1828 when he was in England. But it is his more familiar prints from The Birds of America—the eastern bluebird, cedar waxwing, yellow-shafted flicker, wild turkey, and red-winged blackbird—that visitors admire. Two cases of stuffed birds and mammals and another case displaying prints from his last work, The Viviparous Quadrupeds of North America, fill the room.

Across the hall in two connecting rooms are more bird prints—including the common loon, blue jay, and house wren—a mineral collection, and numerous "Birds in Porcelain" by the noted artist Edward Marshall Boehm. Upstairs the Harding mural continues in a room that also contains more framed Audubon prints, samples of his copperplate engravings, and a picture of the house in France, "La Gerbetiere," where Audubon was raised. A Victorian and a Pennsylvania Dutch bedroom are charming departures from the museum atmosphere of the rest of the house, but the attic, restored as a studio and taxidermy room, recalls the dual focus of Mill Grove as both a museum and wildlife sanctuary dedicated to the memory of John James Audubon.

After a thorough study of Audubon's work inside the house, it is time to explore the world of nature that inspired him. Pick up an illustrated trail map at the office and, at the end of the driveway across from the house, follow the sign that says "To Green Trail." Green Trail is a mile-long loop that begins at the twin bridges. Take a steep left after you cross the bridges. This trail leads up through a grove of hemlock and American beech trees and provides a sweeping view of the Perkiomen 120 feet below. The trail is eroded in places, and the beech trees badly disfigured by aspiring wood carvers, but if you are quiet you will hear a medley of birdcalls from the woods and the creek and glimpse gray squirrels and eastern chipmunks running over the ground.

Shortly after you turn right on Green Trail, you will pass an old chimney, the site of a lead mine that was supposed to make the place profitable for Audubon's father but was instead the first of Audubon's numerous disastrous business ventures. Another right turn takes you past the unmarked graves of the miners, a second-growth woods overhung with vines and dense with underbrush on the right, and a view through the trees of the housing development built up to the property line on the left. Finally, you plunge back into woods on both sides before reaching the twin bridges and returning to the house and parking lot.

There is no picnicking on the grounds, but at the office ask for directions to Lower Perkiomen Valley Park, where you can picnic while enjoying an excellent view of Mill Grove set high on the hill.

The best months to visit Mill Grove are April, May, and October. In spring the large, well-kept apple orchard is in bloom, and the woods support Dutchman's-breeches, spring beauties, jack-in-the-pulpits, mertensia, lesser celandine, bloodroot, and white trilliums. The fall color is at its height in mid-October, and birds are still migrating through on their way south.

Mill Grove is open free of charge from 10:00 A.M. until 4:00 P.M. Tuesday through Saturday and from 1:00 P.M. to 4:00 P.M. on Sundays. Individuals and families are welcome to arrive unannounced, but groups must contact Edward W. Graham, Jr., at the Audubon Wildlife Sanctuary, Audubon, PA 19407 (215-666-5593), and make arrangements for a visit, which includes a guided tour of the house by the director or his assistant. This is an excellent place to take schoolchildren, bird clubs, and Scout troops, but please limit the number to fewer than forty-five people since their facilities can handle no more.

From Philadelphia: Take the Schuylkill Expressway west toward Valley Forge. Shortly before the entrance to the Pennsylvania Turnpike take Exit 26S onto U.S. 202 south toward Paoli. Proceed .5 mile. Exit right onto the Expressway north toward Valley Forge. Follow the Expressway 2.4 miles. Exit onto Pa. 363 north toward Trooper. One-tenth mile from the exit ramp turn left at the first traffic light onto Audubon Road. Follow it 1.2 miles, where it dead-ends on Pawling Road directly in front of the Mill Grove entrance.

19 NOLDE FOREST

When you visit Nolde Forest in Berks County four miles south of Reading, you will be walking through a "Luxury Forest," conceived by its creator, Jacob Nolde, as a source of pleasure rather than of profit. Today this tradition continues since Nolde Forest, now owned by the Bureau of State Parks, is an environmental-education center dedicated to teaching people about the importance of preserving the environment.

In addition to wide-ranging programs aimed at schools or school-related groups, Nolde Forest presents community programs and trains teachers in environmental education. While the office and mansion parking lot are open only on weekdays, the many trails throughout the 666-acre facility are open seven days a week from dawn until dusk.

Once, the land here consisted of unproductive farmland and small scrub hardwoods. That was when Jacob Nolde spotted one lone white pine growing in a meadow. If one pine could grow here, why couldn't others, Nolde wondered. The thought mushroomed into reality when he hired a practical German forester in 1906. Forester Kohout began a massive conifer-planting operation, eventually planting more than 1.5 million white, ponderosa, Scotch, red, Japanese red, and Austrian pines, Norway spruces, Douglas firs, and Japanese larches. Although Jacob lived only ten years after he launched his project, he was well on the way to realizing his hope to "eventually convert a great number of acres of farmland into the most beautiful pine forest in Pennsylvania."

Today you can wander through coniferous plantations of white pine, red pine, Norway spruce, and Douglas fir, or along trails that follow Punches Run, the property's major water source. Watershed Trail, which parallels Angelica Creek and then Punches Run, is particularly attractive since much of it passes through a hardwood forest of mixed oaks, red maple, and American beech, with the usual forest-floor growth of seasonal wildflowers. Canada mayflower, skunk cabbage, false Solomon's seal, and jack-in-the-pulpit are just a few of the spring wildflowers. For a month in the summer the downy rattlesnake plantain and spotted wintergreen are in blossom, but you can see the attractive, patterned, green-and-white leaves of both plants most of the year, particularly the spotted wintergreen, which is an evergreen plant.

Nolde Mansion, Nolde Forest

A special teaching device at Nolde Forest is the large bird blind on Watershed Trail, which provides seating so you can comfortably observe the birds and wild animals through small openings without being seen by them. Feeding stations twenty-five feet away along the creek entice wild turkeys, white-tailed deer, raccoons, ring-necked pheasants, cottontail rabbits, and gray squirrels, while bird feeders bring in a wide variety of seed-eating songbirds. Since there is no hunting in Nolde Forest, a tradition begun by the Noldes, the wildlife is often easy to watch if you are quiet.

The lower part of Watershed Trail, where it closely follows Angelica Creek, runs through an interesting flat area dominated by a planting of white pines and a tall understory of Hercules'-club, or angelica tree, with its bristly twigs, enormous compound leaves, and mounds of white blossoms, which in turn are succeeded by heavy clumps of purple berries beloved by cedar waxwings and American robins.

Many of the trails are old roads built by the Nolde family as fire protection and provide easy walking. One of them, Boulevard Trail, leads up to a large rock outcrop with a fine view of Reading when the leaves are off the trees. It also crosses the highest elevation on the property—eight hundred feet.

Another feature of Nolde Forest is two short loop trails accessible by wheelchairs. One of these leads behind the attractive Nolde Mansion, built in 1927 by Jacob's son Hans and his first wife, Peg. English-Tudor style in front and Gothic-castle in back, this house of Bryn Mawr stone, leaded window frames, copper downspouts, and unique wrought-iron work, including a witch-on-a-broomstick weathervane, supports a roof constructed of two hundred tons of Welsh slate. The landscaping cost the Noldes $40,000; the mansion itself cost approximately $200,000. Then it held a rollicking household of six children; now it is a service center for the Bureau of State Parks. The other loop trail is in the Sawmill area just off Watershed Trail.

The Noldes encouraged horseback riding, and today a horse trail is open around the entire circumference of the property. Part of the trail skirts North Pond, the home of deep-voiced bullfrogs and snapping turtles and an excellent place to observe water-loving wildlife. So is Painted Turtle Pond, near the main entrance road.

Because of the number of well-maintained trails over a relatively gentle terrain, people of all ages can enjoy exploring Nolde Forest year-round.

From Reading: Follow 22, Lancaster Avenue south, .6 mile beyond the intersection of the 422 bypass. Immediately beyond the Reading Railroad overpass, turn left on Pa. 625 and drive for 2.5 miles to the Sawmill entrance. The main entrance is a mile further.

20 DANIEL BOONE HOMESTEAD

For a day rich in American as well as natural history, visit the Daniel Boone Homestead in Berks County near Reading. Owned and administered by the Pennsylvania Historical and Museum Commission, this six-hundred-acre plot has open fields, hedgerows, a small lake, and a wooded nature trail. It is dedicated to the spirit of Daniel Boone, who was born in 1734 in a cabin built on the site, the sixth child of weaver, farmer, and blacksmith Squire Boone.

The trails are open daily from dawn until dusk, but a visitors center and museum are open from 9:00 A.M. until 5:00 P.M. Tuesday through Saturday and from noon until 5:00 P.M. on Sundays. During those times you can also take a tour of the historical buildings.

When you arrive, drive to the parking lot outside the museum and spend some time wandering the gravel trails, which are also used by bicyclists and

Cattail swale and pasture, Daniel Boone Homestead

equestrians. Walk past the Boone Homestead, blacksmith's shop, and Pennsylvania German bank barn, where chickens, goats, and horses live. Below the barn is a cattail swale, and across the trail a marshy hedgerow harbors gray catbirds, eastern phoebes, song sparrows, American goldfinches, American robins, and blue jays in its thick growth of willows, sensitive ferns, asters, goldenrod, thistles, chicory, jewelweed, teasel, ironweed, and evening primrose.

Continue around the curve and look up to your right at the Bertolet log cabin and bake oven. Immediately behind them are horse trails that meander through woods and shrubs. In wet weather much of the trail is churned up by horses' hooves, so good footwear is essential. However, this area, which leads to the upper end of the lake, is filled with wildlife, especially bobwhite quail, and on the lake itself painted turtles bask on rocks. You can either keep left on the trail until you reach the lower stream ford and splash across it to the other side, or you can turn left and follow the lake up past the Deturk cemetery (whose old gravestones have lost their carvings due to acid rain) and the

Bertolet sawmill (where picnic tables are available) and take the paved road back to the parking lot.

There is a fee for a guided tour of the historical buildings, but it is worth it if you are interested in eighteenth-century Pennsylvania pioneer history. Daniel Boone's Homestead was actually built by a later owner, but there is evidence that the foundation of the Boone log house formed part of the foundation wall of the present house. There is also no doubt that Daniel Boone spent the first sixteen years of his life on this land, raising cattle for his father, making friends with the Shawnees, and learning to live on the land as lightly and as well as the Indians.

After your tour, pick up the Daniel Boone Homestead Nature Trail Guide at the visitors center before driving out past the Wayside Lodge and turning right on a paved road. The road leads past two parking lots on your right before it becomes gravel and dead-ends at a third lot. An excellent, half-mile, self-guided nature trail has been built through a patch of woods and is well labeled. With the brochure, you can follow along, bearing right and stopping at each number to learn the names as well as the uses of such trees and shrubs as white oak, white ash, chokecherry, alternate-leaf dogwood, eastern red cedar, hop hornbeam, red maple, Virginia pine, poison oak, and shagbark hickory. The white oak is a magnificent old tree, but the shagbark hickory, which is seventy-five feet tall and 150 years old, is even more impressive. Other trail features are an anthill; remnants of chestnut fencing; small, hidden animal trails; and a woodchuck den. Owl pellets and piles of feathers on the trail are evidence of predators as well as prey.

Because of the mild climate, any season is a good one to explore Daniel Boone's Homestead, but spring and fall are the best. By calling ahead (215-582-4900), groups can be accommodated on tours. It is an excellent place to take schoolchildren or Scout troops so they can see where Daniel Boone spent his formative years as a Quaker; as an adopted son of Blackfish, the chief of a Shawnee tribe; and as a reluctant cattle raiser, always slipping off to try his wilderness skills instead of learning the more prosaic pioneer crafts.

From Reading: At the intersection of Route 22 with Lancaster Avenue, take 422 east for 7.8 miles until you reach a light and the intersection with Route 82. Continue ahead for 3.1 miles until you see a sign on the right for Daniel Boone Homestead. Turn left onto Daniel Boone Road for .9 mile until you enter the Homestead property; then follow the paved road until you reach the visitors center.

21 HAWK MOUNTAIN SANCTUARY

Ask any birdwatcher in the world what Pennsylvania has to offer and chances are he or she will answer, "Hawk Mountain." Described by Hawk Mountain's first caretaker, Maurice Broun, in his book *Hawks Aloft,* as "the crossroads of naturalists," this 2,185-acre sanctuary along the Kittatinny Ridge in eastern Pennsylvania's Berks and Schuylkill counties celebrated its golden anniversary in 1984.

On any fall day Hawk Mountain's sandstone outcroppings are crowded with men, women, and children, all armed with binoculars, cameras, and telescopes, raptly watching the migration of thousands of birds of prey. A yearly average of 20,000 raptors of fourteen species pass along the ridge. Beginning in late August, and continuing through September, huge kettles of broad-winged hawks often swirl over the mountain. On September 14, 1978, an all-time high for broad-wings occurred—21,448—and those who saw the "Miracle Day," as they called it, will never forget it.

But any autumn day with a wind will make a visit worthwhile. Ospreys, American kestrels, and an occasional bald eagle are other September migrants, while October is the month to see large numbers of red-tailed, sharp-shinned, and Cooper's hawks and northern harriers. November is golden-eagle month, though red-tailed hawks are still passing over in large numbers, along with occasional sharp-shinned, rough-legged, red-shouldered, and Cooper's hawks.

In the woods along the rocky trail to the mountaintop, you are liable to see an array of songbirds. Since 1934 over 246 species of birds have been identified at the sanctuary. Wildflowers are abundant in the spring, and mountain laurel and rhododendron put on a show in June and early July. White-tailed deer, masked shrews, long-tailed weasels, eastern chipmunks, and black bears also live on Hawk Mountain.

Start at the visitors center, which is open 8:00 A.M. to 5:00 P.M. daily except Thanksgiving, Christmas, and New Year's Day. At the center are excellent exhibits on raptors, information about the sanctuary's history, a gift shop filled with nature books and wildlife art prints, and a place to sit and watch the birds at the outdoor feeders just beyond the large observation window. There, too, you can stock up on water to accompany the picnic lunch you are allowed to eat up on the rocks.

Make your first stop at South Lookout. Sometimes, if the wind is right, there are good sightings here. But most birders press on to North Lookout, where the open outcropping of Tuscarora sandstone gives visitors a seventy-mile vista of mountains and valleys. At 1,521 feet above sea level, the slope falls almost straight off for a thousand feet to the Little Schuylkill River below.

North Lookout, Hawk Mountain Sanctuary (Photo by Theodora Kreitz)

Find yourself a free rock among a crowd of expert birders, and if you don't know your birds very well, listen and learn. Someone will call out every bird of prey long before you spot it. In between sightings you can admire the scarlet berries of the mountain ash that grows between the rocks; look for the blue-tailed skinks living there; or examine the intertwining, radiating ridges on the rocks, fossilized burrowings of the large seaworm Arthrophycus, which lived on the sandy bottom of what was the Silurian Sea half a billion years ago.

Back in 1932 life was especially precarious for the thousands of birds of prey that sailed south along the ridge from September through November. Conservation crusader Rosalie Edge visited the mountain that fall with Richard Pough, a concerned Philadelphia news photographer, and there they witnessed, from every sandstone outcropping along the ridge, the wholesale slaughter of birds of prey by armed men. Hawks were "wanton killers," those men believed, and by shooting them they were performing a service for humanity. Rosalie Edge did not agree. As head of the newly formed Emergency Conservation Committee, she swung into action. Through her efforts the killing was stopped; a portion of the mountain was purchased in 1934 (at $2.50 an acre) as a private sanctuary; and Hawk Mountain, the best known of all the natural areas in our state, "a glider highway," as Richard Pough called it, was saved for posterity.

Many years of patrolling the mountain and confronting trespassers bent on killing hawks lay ahead for caretaker Maurice Broun and his wife, Irma. In addition, they, and members of the privately maintained Hawk Mountain Sanctuary, faced the monumental task of educating the public about the ecological niche occupied by birds of prey. Theirs was the first sanctuary in the world to offer protection to migrating hawks and eagles. Over several decades, the Hawk Mountain Association managed to obtain its two goals, "to create a sympathetic understanding for birds of prey and to further interest in their conservation." Today these goals have been extended to encompass all wildlife in an effort "to create [a] better understanding of man's relationship to the environment."

A brisk fall day is the best time to vist Hawk Mountain. Weekends are crowded, so a weekday is best. Numerous year-round educational programs reach their peak during the autumn, with a lecture series each Saturday evening as well as natural-history and conservation trail lectures. Nonmembers are charged a small fee to take the three-quarter-mile trail to North Lookout.

The Hawk Mountain Association presents programs for groups throughout the year; reservations are necessary (call 215-756-6961). Special workshops, trips, and seasonal events like the annual Winterfest are open to everyone, although association members usually receive first priority and special discounts.

Hawk Mountain is *the* place to be for naturalists during a Pennsylvania autumn. Take at least one day then to join the nature lovers who flock here each year to witness the spectacular migration of birds.

From Reading: Take Pa. Route 61 north approximately 24 miles. Turn right on Pa. Route 895. Proceed 2 miles to Drehersville. Turn right at the sign and go up the steep mountain road for a mile. A parking lot and visitors center are on your right.

22 THE NOTTINGHAM SERPENTINE BARRENS

The Nottingham Serpentine Barrens in southwestern Chester County is one of two substantial serpentine barrens left in the state. Because the greenish serpentine rock is a good road-building stone, most of the original two dozen serpentine barrens in Pennsylvania have been mined out. But, so far, 693 acres of the 1,000-acre Goat Hill Barrens, also in southwestern Chester County, have been saved by the Nature Conservancy, while Chester County itself purchased the six-mile-long, two-mile-wide Nottingham Barrens for a county park in 1962.

The Goat Hill Barrens, with 600 acres now owned by the Pennsylvania Department of Environmental Resources and the remaining 93 acres by the Nature Conservancy, is open to the public but there are no trails. Nottingham Park, on the other hand, has eight miles of horseback and hiking trails, year-round camping facilities, picnic areas with pavilions, two large fishing ponds, and playgrounds.

Best of all, though, is the portion of the park (more than half of its 651 acres) that has been designated as a Chester County Natural Area. It features rare plants, unusual bird species, a large forest of pitch pine underlaid with an almost impenetrable greenbrier barrier, and numerous rock formations and abandoned feldspar and chrome quarries.

At the first parking lot take the yellow-blazed Chrome Trail, which joins the white-blazed Doe Trail after eight hundred feet. In April an assortment of unusual wildflowers will be growing along the edges of the trail and on the serpentine outcroppings. Probably the most spectacular, although not the rarest, of the flowers will be masses of moss pink in three distinctive shades— light, medium, and dark pink—as well as the endemic white serpentine chickweeds with handsome, dime-sized flowers and fuzzy, grayish-green leaves. Lyre-leaved rock cress, spring beauty, early saxifrage, and dwarf cinquefoil are also common, while skunk cabbage graces the banks of Black Run.

In late summer and early fall other unusual wildflowers growing here include the serpentine or depauperate aster (another endemic species known only from three Pennsylvania counties and one in Maryland), the white-flowered whorled milkweed, and the sunbright, or fameflower, which has pink flowers that last only one day. In fact, fameflower reaches its northern limit here. Also look closely for the Aleutian maidenhair fern, a disjunct species, meaning that it grows far from the rest of its population in Canada and Alaska. Another disjunct species, Small's ragwort, is found north of Virginia only on serpentine outcrops. These species, like the other plants and trees here, prefer the dry, sandy, mineral-poor soil of a serpentine barren.

Overlook along Buck Trail, Nottingham Serpentine Barrens

Eventually Doe Trail meets the red-blazed Buck Trail. Turn right and follow it until it intersects Lonesome Pine Trail, where you take another right and head northwest back toward the parking lot. Some of the trails are not well marked, so you may not end up exactly where you started, but if you make two right turns you should be able to find your way through the barrens. Because of the impenetrable greenbrier, it is impossible to wander off the trails.

The birds are also unusual for this region of the state. Seventeen species of warblers breed here, including the prairie, yellow-throated (normally a more southerly species), pine, and cerulean. Broad-winged hawks wheel overhead, and whippoorwills and bobwhite quail are common.

Even the wild grasses are noteworthy—little bluestem, Indian grass, and grama grass—all originally western prairie species. And the extensive forest of pitch pine is one of the largest in the state.

Since the trails are wide and rolling, it is easy to walk several miles, especially in early spring while it is still cool. The combination of an unusual natural environment with abundant recreational opportunities makes Nottingham Park an excellent place for group as well as family outings.

From Lancaster: From the center of the city follow Route 222 (Prince Street) south. At the traffic light 3.8 miles from center city, continue straight ahead on Route 272 south. Turn left off the main highway at Wakefield, 20.6 miles from downtown Lancaster, and continue to follow 272 toward Nottingham. Between Wakefield and Nottingham are few 272 signs, so watch for the following route characteristics given in miles from Wakefield: .7, continue straight ahead; 3.2, continue straight ahead at the stop sign; 3.4, the road to Nottingham continues straight; 7.3, the road to Nottingham bears right; 9.1, cross over U.S. 1 and continue straight ahead into the town. At the stop sign make a sharp right; a sign indicates Nottingham Park. Turn right again .4 mile further and follow the road another .9 mile to the park entrance on the left.

23 MIDDLE CREEK WILDLIFE MANAGEMENT AREA

Each spring birdwatchers from all over the eastern part of the state make their first outing—in mid-March—to Middle Creek Wildlife Management Area on the Lebanon-Lancaster county border to observe migrating waterfowl. This Pennsylvania Game Commission impoundment of Middle Creek, which was constructed in 1966, has created ideal nesting and feeding habitat for waterfowl out of what was originally marshy ground with only marginal agricultural possibilities.

Since the money used to buy and develop the land came from a $70 million bond issue (called Project 70) approved by Pennsylvania voters in 1963, as well as from a second bond issue (Project 500), the Game Commission believes Middle Creek should serve all citizens, and not just hunters. So there are picnic areas, hiking and nature trails, an excellent interpretive area at the visitors center, an auto tour to follow to see the maximum number of waterfowl, and opportunities to fish, boat, bike, ride horseback, birdwatch, and hunt.

As soon as you enter the five-thousand-acre property, you can see (and hear) Middle Creek's most successful propagation project, the Canada goose. In 1969 thirty mated pairs from the Game Commission's Pymatuning facility, as well as a few nuisance geese and others bought from licensed propagators, were released. Fifteen years later the resident population was in excess of four thousand geese, despite a limited hunting season. They breed in Middle Creek's many inlets, ponds, and potholes, wander over its cornfields, and swim on the four-hundred-acre lake.

View along Conservation Trail, Middle Creek Wildlife Management Area

While Canada geese are the facility's main, year-round attraction, alert birdwatchers can also pick out nesting wood ducks, mallards, black ducks, blue-winged teal, northern shovelers, and hooded mergansers, all of which use the many kinds of nesting boxes designed by the Game Commission. These include straw rolled into a cylinder of chicken wire on a stake about a foot above shallow water (preferred by mallards), old rubber tires affixed to tree stumps a yard above water level (used by Canada geese), and metal cylinders with conical roofs or wooden boxes (attractive to wood ducks).

The first place to stop at Middle Creek is the handsome visitors center. Set on a small hill and with a large picture window overlooking the lake, the center is open from 9:00 A.M. until 4:00 P.M. (except Mondays) March 1 through November 30. Here you can pick up maps and brochures about Middle Creek before studying the mounted and clearly labeled birds of prey, waterfowl, and songbirds. The mammals of Middle Creek form another display, and wild turkeys, ring-necked pheasants, and other game birds are placed in habitat settings.

Next take the auto tour, but be sure to park and hike the flat, 2,500-foot-long Willow Point Trail out to an observation point that overlooks a portion of the lake (the second stop). Here, if you are lucky, you will see many species of waterfowl: Snow geese, tundra swans, common loons, common pintails, gadwalls, American widgeons, redheads, canvasbacks, buffleheads, old-squaws, greater and lesser scaups, ring-necked ducks, all three merganser species, common goldeneyes, and green-winged teals are just some of the possibilities.

Drive slowly and scan all the small ponds, but also keep alert overhead since golden and bald eagles and broad-winged, rough-legged, red-tailed, and red-shouldered hawks are often spotted here, especially during migration. In the sloughs you are liable to glimpse common, snowy, and cattle egrets; great blue, little blue, green-backed, and black-crowned night herons; American and least bitterns; Virginia, sora, and king rails; and a wide variety of plovers and sandpipers. Even gulls—herring, ring-billed, and Bonaparte's—soar over the water in spring and fall.

After following the auto tour, which makes a wide circle of the lake, park at the Sunfish Pond Picnic Area, just below the visitors center, and walk the 1.4-mile Conservation Trail. This circular trail passes through a variety of upland habitats managed by the Game Commission for white-tailed deer, ruffed grouse, bobwhite quail, ring-necked pheasants, and cottontail rabbits. Many of the trees are labeled, and there are several interpretive signs. This is also a good place to see some of the songbirds that live in the wooded areas of Middle Creek.

A more rugged hike, the Millstone Trail, leads to a mountain-crest vista and an old millstone quarry. A connecting path joins Horseshoe Trail, a segment of the 121-mile horseback and hiking trail that starts near Valley Forge and ends at a junction near Harrisburg with the Appalachian Trail. Deer Path Nature Trail and Valley View, Middle Creek, and Elder Run trails also provide interesting, easy hiking.

March and October are probably the best times to visit Middle Creek, but wildlife is abundant year-round: 238 bird species have been identified, as well as muskrats, woodchucks, red and gray foxes, raccoons, white-tailed deer, skunks, gray squirrels, cottontail rabbits, and opossums.

Middle Creek Wildlife Management Area was created by man to manage wildlife, and it has been successful. Although it is in no way a wilderness area, it is a haven for wild creatures often hard-pressed by man's mismanagement of the land. In a country that usually sees wetlands as wastelands to be drained and developed, the Game Commission's creation of such a habitat is to be commended.

From Lancaster (Pa. 283 exit north of the city): Take Route 501 for 17 miles north to Schaefferstown. Turn right and follow Pa. 897 east 3 miles to Kleinfeltersville. In the center of the village turn right on Hopeland Road (the only paved right turn), which leads directly into Middle Creek Wildlife Management Area.

CENTRAL PENNSYLVANIA

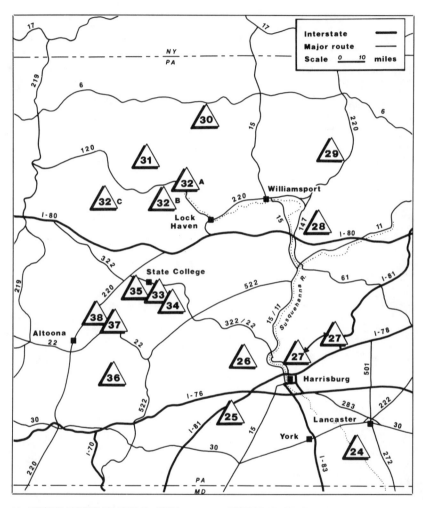

24 OTTER CREEK NATURAL AREA

The Otter Creek Natural Area, on the west bank of the lower Susquehanna River south of York, is a small portion of the five-thousand-acre property owned by Pennsylvania Power and Light Company on both sides of the river between Safe Harbor Dam in the north and Holtwood Dam in the south. Because of the dams, this section of the river has been renamed Lake Aldred, and PP&L has provided for a wide range of recreational activities, including boating, fishing, hunting, camping, picnicking, and hiking, in the area.

Many days could be spent exploring PP&L land, but the most spectacular natural places are the hemlock-lined Otter Creek gorge and the path along the river leading to the Urey Overlook. Both areas are rich in wildflowers, birds, and mammals, and Otter Creek itself has one of the largest virgin-timber tracts in the Piedmont province of the central Atlantic states.

Park outside the office of the Otter Creek Campgrounds, which are open all year, and take the half-mile-long Nature Trail that winds through the gorge and back up to the campground. Or, if you have good hiking shoes and some stamina, follow the red blazes along the creek for another half mile until you reach a ford. Then you can either retrace your steps through the gorge or wade the creek, continue on the red-blazed trail for a short distance until it reaches Pa. 425, and turn right on that road back to the campground.

Since the land has been clear-cut just over the natural-area line on state game lands, it is best to stay down in the steep, rock-filled gorge, where the stream, with its small waterfalls and enormous hemlock, tulip, and sycamore trees, is much the same as it was when settlers first moved into the area and began burning trees for charcoal to fuel the York Iron Furnace near the mouth of the creek. Remnants of the furnace can still be seen, the only signs of humanity other than the litter that occasionally mars the trail.

Many of the boulders in the gorge are beautiful ferneries, with evergreen wood, Christmas, and common polypody ferns. Although most of the rocks consist of gray-flecked schist, in one section magnificent, sparkling white

Otter Creek Gorge, Otter Creek Natural Area

quartzite outcroppings can be seen.

Belted kingfishers nest in a muddy bank along the creek, while eastern phoebes have reverted from manmade structures to their ancestral dwellings under rock ledges. In the woods above the trail, bloodroot, mayapples, skunk cabbage, Canada mayflowers, trout lilies, and jack-in-the-pulpit bloom in the spring. Umbrella magnolia shrubs, usually a more southerly species and noted for their long, wide leaves, large cream-colored blossoms, and beautiful rose-colored fruit, grow in the understory.

Because Otter Creek Trail is narrow and slippery in places, it must be explored slowly and with care. But the yellow-blazed trail along the river, called the Urey Trail, which begins just over the bridge on Pa. 425 directly below the campground, is flat for the first half mile and leads through a magnificent river-bottomland woods thick with wildflowers in April and May. Large white, painted, and purple trilliums, Dutchman's-breeches, Virginia bluebells (mertensia), and cut-leaved toothworts are especially abundant, and along the short but very steep ascent to the Urey Lookout tiny bluets bloom on either side of the trail.

On a clear day the view of the five Urey Islands to the south and Weise Island to the northwest is worth the effort to get there. My husband and I were further rewarded in early April by hearing the gobbling of a wild turkey just over the rise. After sitting and listening to him gobble for well over a half hour, we plunged into the woods from where the sound emanated and had a glimpse of him as he flew off over the river.

You can follow a gentler yellow-blazed descent down the hill and then take a short right to reach Pa. 425. Then cross the road and pick up a portion of the red-blazed trail on the other side of Otter Creek. On this short, easy-to-walk loop, you can hear but not see the creek below until you reach the road bridge that crosses the creek. From there it is only a few hundred feet back to the campground.

From Memorial Day to Labor Day, when all the facilities are open and a full-time naturalist is in residence, there are many places where you can park and walk short stretches along the river. Another possibility, from mid-April until mid-October, is to turn right on Pa. 425 when you leave the campground and follow the signs to the Indian Steps Historic Area (also owned by PP&L). Originally built by York County lawyer John Edward Vandersloot, who collected Indian artifacts, this fine museum of Eastern Indian arrowheads is now open to the public. On the grounds outside, which overlook the river, a short, self-guided walking tour has been designed especially for older people by one of the Otter Creek directors, Fern Entrekin.

No matter what your age or capabilities, you will enjoy a visit to the Otter Creek Natural Area and its environs. For hiking maps and other information, write to George R. Aukamp, Lake Superintendent, PP&L, R.D. 3, Box 345, Holtwood, PA 17532, or call 717-284-2278.

From York (Interstate 83, Exit 6E): Follow Pa. 74 for 11 miles south through Dallastown and Red Lion. Turn left onto a country road, where a sign points to New Bridgeville and Craley. Another sign before the road sign indicates Otter

Creek Recreation Area. Proceed 2.9 miles to New Bridgeville and turn right on Pa.
425 (another sign points to Otter Creek). Drive about 6 miles; then go down a very
steep hill (recreational vehicles proceed with caution) to Otter Creek Recreation
Area. Parking (and maps) is at the campground office up an incline to the right.
Parking in season is at parking lots on the left.

25 KINGS GAP ENVIRONMENTAL EDUCATION CENTER

Kings Gap Environmental Education Center, ten miles south of Carlisle in
Cumberland County, is owned by the Pennsylvania Department of Environmental Resources and operated by the Bureau of State Parks. One of four
environmental education centers operated by the DER (Nolde Forest is another), Kings Gap attracts thirty thousand people yearly to its special programs for schoolchildren, families, and teachers, as well as to its fifteen miles
of trails.

A long, winding road from the base of South Mountain to its summit leads
to the old Cameron mansion, which houses the Education Center. Built in
1907, the stone, cement, and brick structure is virtually fireproof. It served as
a summer home for James Cameron until 1952, when it was purchased by the
C. H. Masland Carpet Company as a guesthouse for prospective clients.

The mansion had been decorated in wealthy hunting-lodge style—hanging
Belgian tapestries, Oriental rugs, and heavy, overstuffed, comfortable furniture
upholstered in leather—but Masland made it a showcase for their high-
quality wool rugs, rugs so durable that they still are used in the mansion.

Architecturally the mansion is not particularly attractive, but the view out
over the mountains and the Cumberland Valley from the open terrace is worth
the visit. Also, you can pick up trail maps and literature about Kings Gap at
the office, which is open from 8:00 A.M. until 4:00 P.M. Monday through
Friday and on weekends when programs are scheduled.

Kings Gap, including the mansion and its furnishings, was sold to the DER
through the Nature Conservancy in 1973. After being used as a training center
for DER employees for a few years, the 2,600-acre property was opened up as
an environmental education center in 1977. Since then both programs and
trails have steadily proliferated, and new ideas are continually pursued in an
effort to teach people not only about nature but about the early history of the
area. Both self-guided historical trails and self-guided nature trails abound on
the property. The former include Charcoal Hearth Trail, with interpretive

Allegheny ant mound, Kings Gap Environmental Education Center

signs explaining the reconstructed charcoal mound, barren charcoal hearths, and old roads used for hauling charcoal. At the base of the mountain is a restored log house.

For those interested in nature, probably the most rewarding series of trails includes the Ant Mound, a short section of the Boundary, and the Watershed self-guided nature trails, a circular walk over easy terrain that covers 1.8 miles. Park in the Pond Parking Area on your right halfway up the winding mountain road. From there an easy one-tenth-mile trail leads you to Watershed Trail. Turn left on that white-blazed trail and follow it for six-tenths of a mile as it winds upstream beside Kings Gap Run. Interpretive signs along the way explain what a watershed is. Large chunks of quartzite in the stream turn the water a milky white in places, and the moist areas support impressive stands of cinnamon, royal, and interrupted ferns along with mats of sphagnum moss and twinflowers.

A highlight along this trail is a large, hollow black gum tree. Peer up into its interior to see its intricate spiral shape. There are also numerous clumps of the wildflower fly poison, which likes sandy woods and blooms from May through

July. A member of the lily family, fly poison boasts showy white clusters of six-petaled flowers that turn dull green to purplish as they age.

When you reach the blue-blazed Boundary Trail, turn right and follow it for four-tenths of a mile; then make a right onto the brown-blazed Ant Mound Trail. Almost immediately you will see more fly poison. The ant mounds, which were also visible on Boundary Trail, become even larger. These mounds were built by the Allegheny mound-building ant (*Formica exsectoides*) in the sandy soil they need to erect their unique homes. The ants build in an open, sunny spot since moss, which grows in shady woods, might otherwise gradually encircle a mound and cover it, smothering the up to 55,000 ants that may occupy a single mound.

The ants, headed by a fertile queen and consisting of some males and a large number of sterile workers, also kill any young trees within fifty feet of their mound by biting them. The formic acid their mouths exude prevents the downward flow of plant nutrients, effectively eliminating any trees from two to fifteen years old that might shade their mounds and create an ideal environment for moss to grow.

The mounds begin as craters and become two-foot-high hills as the worker ants carry debris, piece by piece, to pile on top of the crater. The Allegheny mound-building ants live mainly on honeydew produced by aphids, supplementing that sweet diet with insects.

Rufous-sided towhees, common yellowthroats, gray catbirds, and wood pewees sing and call in the surrounding woods. The trail is wide and well graveled, the perfect sunning spot for a northern copperhead I discovered during my visit there in midsummer. But it kept its distance just as I kept mine, flattening its coppery-red head before slithering off into the woods, and providing a good reason for staying on the trail as well as an exciting climax to my walk.

When you reach Watershed Trail again, thus completing the circular route, make a short detour left to the small pond, where dragonflies zoom over the water. Incidentally, just above the parking lot is a paved trail for the handicapped.

Kings Gap Environmental Center is best visited in the summer if you are interested in ferns, fly poison, and watching the ants at work, but the wide variety of Family Nature Days held on many weekends is a drawing card throughout the year. For special group outings, call 717-486-5031 or write Kings Gap Environmental Education and Training Center, 500 Kings Gap Road, Carlisle, PA 17013, several months ahead of the date you are hoping to reserve (but be prepared to accept an alternate since the center's director, Hilary Vida, and his staff maintain a busy schedule). There are no picnic facilities at Kings Gap, because the focus is on natural and historical education rather than on recreation, so it is a good idea to bring along snacks that can be eaten as you walk.

From Harrisburg: Follow any of the major highways west to Carlisle: the Pennsylvania Turnpike, U.S. 11, or Interstate 81 south. Connect to Pa. Route 34 south out of Carlisle. Follow Route 34 for 3.8 miles south of the intersection with Interstate 81. Turn right on Pine Road. Drive 5.4 miles to entrance on the left to Kings Gap.

26 BOX HUCKLEBERRY NATURAL AREA

If you want to see the oldest plant in the world, forget the redwood forests of California and the twisted bristlecone pines of the Sierra. Visit instead the Box Huckleberry Natural Area in Pennsylvania's Tuscarora State Forest near New Bloomfield.

There you will find a nine-acre sanctuary with a well-marked trail leading past white pine, white oak, and red maple trees and smooth sumac and mountain laurel bushes. It is an easy, restful walk, highlighted by a lovely, rare, evergreen blueberry plant, the box huckleberry (*Gaylussacia brachycera*). Forming an attractive ground cover with its boxwood-like, gleaming leaves, box huckleberry is especially appealing in May and early June when its pink and white flowers appear.

Although its great age wasn't discovered until this century, box huckleberry previously gained fame of sorts among botanists because of its rarity. In 1796 the French naturalist Andre Michaux first discovered box huckleberry in the vicinity of what is now West Virginia, but no one else had seen it when the great botanist Asa Gray began his monumental *Manual of the Botany of the Northern United States* (better known as *Gray's Manual of Botany*) in the 1840s. Then, just as Gray was readying his book for the press, he received a letter from a young, unknown Dickinson College professor, Spencer Fullerton Baird, which reported his discovery of box huckleberry near his home in Carlisle, Pennsylvania.

Baird was an accomplished naturalist as well as an inspiring biology professor. As a youth, he had discovered a new bird, the least flycatcher, which he had sent to John James Audubon, thus becoming a protégé of the famous ornithologist-artist. Similarly, his rediscovery of box huckleberry impressed Asa Gray; later, Gray's enthusiastic endorsement of Baird helped him to secure a position as assistant secretary of the Smithsonian Institution. Baird

Box huckleberry and lichens, Box Huckleberry Natural Area

went on to become the illustrious second Secretary of the Smithsonian as well as the founder of the U.S. Fish Commission.

Even long after Baird's death in 1888, the box huckleberry was still known as simply a rare plant. However, in 1919, F. V. Coville of the U.S. Department of Agriculture, who had been studying the New Bloomfield box-huckleberry patch, made an electrifying discovery. The New Bloomfield patch was a single plant that was more than a thousand years old! The plant, he maintained, had spread by rhizomes at a rate of six inches per year; thus it had taken more than ten centuries to spread across those nine acres.

Until then, only one other box-huckleberry colony, a ten-foot-square area in Delaware, had been found. But after Coville's announcement, the search for older colonies was on. In 1920 H. A. Ward of Harrisburg discovered a much larger site, near Losh Run, thirty miles from New Bloomfield. That colony was twelve thousand years old! Subsequently, other discoveries of the plant were made in Maryland, Virginia, West Virginia, Kentucky, and Tennessee, but none was as old as the Losh Run site. Unfortunately, that locality was ruined by the rebuilding of U.S. 22–322, so the only place in Pennsylvania to see the box huckleberry in an undisturbed environment is at the New Bloomfield location.

You are likely to find yourself alone when you visit the Box Huckleberry Natural Area, which is a National Natural Landmark, and you can wander the quiet quarter-mile-long trail following signs that guide you around the box-huckleberry patch. Since it has evergreen leaves of shiny, dark green, box huckleberry remains an attractive plant even in winter.

In spring this area is lovely with the blossoms of flowering dogwoods, wild azaleas, shadbush, and mountain laurel. False Solomon's seal, pink lady's slipper, rue anemone, wild pink, perfoliate bellwort, and other woodland wildflowers are also in blossom then.

Summer is dominated by the ghostly white of Indian pipes and the large, seedy fruit of the box huckleberry. Growing next to it in several places is lowbush blueberry, with its light green leaves that are shed in autumn. With the two species growing side by side, it is easy to see the difference in leaves between them. Occasional butterflies, like the great spangled fritillary, flutter by, and off in the woods the slow, plaintive songs of eastern pewees can be heard.

In autumn the box huckleberry has a red tinge to its leaves, the jack-in-the-pulpit's red-berried stalk lights up the forest floor, and the deciduous trees take on glowing fall colors.

This is an excellent place to take a garden club since the trail is short and easy. For youth groups, camping overnight in nearby Colonel Denning State Park with a side trip to the Box Huckleberry Natural Area would be worthwhile, especially if the botanical history of the place is explained by knowledgeable leaders ahead of time.

From Harrisburg: Cross the Susquehanna River on the Camp Hill Bridge (Forster Street). Turn north on U.S. 11–15. Proceed 14 miles to the junction of Pa. 274 at the edge of Duncannon. Turn left. Go 7 miles west on 274 to intersection with Pa. 34. Turn right on 274–34 north toward New Bloomfield. Proceed 2.3 miles. Turn

left and left again after 600 feet onto Huckleberry Road. Drive about .5 mile to the
Box Huckleberry Natural Area. Park at the edge of the road below the small sign
that identifies the sanctuary on the hillside to your left.

27 STONY CREEK VALLEY

If you want to see ruffed grouse in abundance, head for Stony Creek Valley,
State Game Lands 211, on a clear, cool autumn day. Located north of
Harrisburg in Dauphin and Lebanon counties, Stony Creek Valley is twenty
miles long and a half mile wide and is tucked between Sharp and Stony
mountains on the north and Second Mountain on the south. The old, abandoned Schuylkill and Susquehanna Railroad bed provides easy, flat walking
the entire length of the valley and can be entered from either the east or west
end.

This valley had once been active with coal mining and lumbering opera-
tions, and the railroad had serviced a few small towns like Rausch Gap and
Yellow Springs. Now such places are ghost towns, and the railroad bed is
closed to all motorized vehicles. Concerned individuals worked hard to keep
Stony Creek a totally wild, roadless area. As a result, it is easy to imagine when
you visit this area that you have been propelled back to pre-settler days in
Pennsylvania, especially when you leave the railroad bed and make forays
down to the hemlock-lined banks of Stony Creek, where not even a footpath
mars the wilderness.

In addition to grouse, there are gray squirrels, wild turkeys, white-tailed
deer, cottontail rabbits, and red foxes. Rumor has it that it is even possible to
see bobcats and coyotes here. While game birds are certainly plentiful, so are
songbirds and birds of prey. Pileated woodpeckers, ruby-crowned kinglets,
white-throated sparrows, northern juncos, red-tailed hawks, American goldfinches, cedar waxwings, and red-bellied woodpeckers are just a few of the
birds you can see in the fall.

Along either side of the trail at its eastern end, several species of ferns—
including lacy-looking lady ferns; enormous, plume-shaped ostrich ferns; and
locust-leaf-like royal ferns—grow in wet areas that also support sphagnum
moss and sharp-edged sedges. Interrupted, sensitive, and cinnamon ferns are
also abundant, and on the large rocks common polypody ferns can sometimes
be found.

Several species of autumn wildflowers thrive in the ditches along the old
railroad bed as well. White wood asters, white snakeroot, silverrod, downy

Old railroad bridge over Rausch Creek, Stony Creek Valley

lobelia, Indian tobacco, and assorted species of goldenrod prefer the dry stretches, while the lovely, blue closed gentians grow in the moist places.

Numerous narrow foot trails intersect the railroad bed. The more adventurous can ascend Water Tank Trail up a steep path to the top of Sharp Mountain and over to the Stony Mountain Fire Tower, or they can take portions of the Horseshoe Trail, the Yellow Springs Trail, or the Appalachian Trail that cross the main trail.

In addition to young forest, there are places where white pines and hemlocks dominate the landscape. Sand Spring is situated in one such place, less than two miles from the eastern end of the valley. The old hemlocks create a dense shade on the warmest summer day, and the needle-carpeted ground is amply supplied with large, flat rocks. Icy spring water runs out of the hillside and into a small, still pool, lowering the air temperature by a good ten degrees. Black-capped chickadees and wood thrushes scold as you enter their sanctuary; otherwise the only sound you hear is the trickle of water over small stones.

Another detour can be made at the old stone railroad bridge, where Rausch

Run crosses the trail along with the Appalachian Trail. If you turn south on the Appalachian Trail, you will be able to find both an old cemetery and the clear beginnings of Stony Creek just beneath the plank bridge. Hike a short way down along the creek to see some magnificent, large hardwood trees growing in a wet area of sphagnum moss and sedges.

If you tire of woods, the Game Commission has mowed several fields scattered throughout State Game Lands 211. One five-acre plot, a couple hundred feet south off the main trail and just a short distance beyond Sand Spring, is a wonderful place to watch wildlife at dawn or dusk.

Every season has its rewards at Stony Creek. Winter brings out cross-country skiers and dogsled enthusiasts. Spring is a good time to find woodland wildflowers and observe migrating warblers. Summer should produce numerous sightings of young families—including those of ruffed grouse, wild turkeys, and white-tailed deer. But autumn, with its tangy air, blue skies, and abundant wildlife, is the most rewarding season of all. (Remember, though, to visit only on Sundays during hunting season.)

You can walk the entire twenty-mile valley in one day if you take two cars and leave one at the further end of the valley so that you can drive back to your point of origin (and other car). Or you can do as we did and walk as far in as you can from each end on two different days.

From Harrisburg (western end): Follow 322–22 west 10 miles to the borough of Dauphin. Exit on 225 north and drive a couple hundred feet across the bridge over Stony Creek. Turn right on Stony Creek Road. (The sign says State Game Lands 8 miles). Follow the paved road for 5 miles and continue ahead on a dirt road until you reach the gate that marks the beginning of the trail.

(eastern end): Follow Interstate 81 north 24 miles to Exit 30, Pa. Route 72. At the stop sign at the end of the exit ramp, turn left and proceed a few hundred yards to the center of town. Turn left at the traffic light. Follow the paved road 2.8 miles to the junction with Route 443. Bear right on 443. Drive 1.5 miles and turn left on Gold Mine Road. Drive over Second Mountain 2.8 miles. Watch for the entrance on the left to State Game Lands 211 and the beginning of the trail.

28 MONTOUR PRESERVE

Montour Preserve, near Danville, is a model of how industry can serve its own needs and still develop a refuge for wild creatures and for people who appreciate the outdoors. Established in 1972 by the Pennsylvania Power and Light

Lake Chillisquaque, Montour Preserve

Company, this thousand-acre preserve protects Lake Chillisquaque, which was created to provide an emergency cooling water supply for PP&L's coal-fired electric-generating plant three miles south of the preserve.

Lake Chillisquaque was named for the middle branch of Chillisquaque Creek, the reservoir's primary tributary, and it is the focal point of Montour Preserve. The 165-acre lake attracts more than fifty species of waterfowl during the peak of spring migration in late March, including, of course, Canada geese. This is only appropriate since the name Chillisquaque comes from an old Indian word, "Chilisuagi," meaning "song of the wild goose." But other waterfowl, including pied-billed grebes, tundra swans, and numerous species of shorebirds, are also in abundance.

Boating and fishing are allowed on the lake, but only canoes, sailboats, and small boats with electric motors are permitted. Since the Pennsylvania Fish Commission stocks the lake, fishermen can pull in such species as northern pike, walleye, tiger muskelunge, largemouth bass, perch, and bluegills. Along the lake are two picnic areas and a 148-acre wildlife refuge with two blinds that can be used for wildlife study and photography after you secure a permit from the preserve office.

The visitors center gives you an overall view of the history, both natural and human, of the Montour Preserve. Here you can see a display of mounted birds of prey, a Lake Chillisquaque fish and wildlife exhibit, bird nests, a slide presentation, and an excellent fossil exhibit, the latter a reminder to visitors that there is a fossil pit on the preserve where fossil buffs are permitted to dig.

Across from the visitors center is the preserve office, a beautifully restored Victorian farmhouse built in 1877. The Laura Smith Trail of History, which leads around the immediate grounds of the home, is named for its last occupant, a granddaughter of the original settlers. This self-guided, twenty-five-minute walk provides a glimpse of an earlier era in farm living by illustrating old building techniques and farm equipment. A charming herb garden and a wildlife pond are also interesting points along the trail.

For the best overview of the natural attractions of Montour Preserve, take the circular four-and-a-quarter-mile Chillisuagi Trail, which begins at the visitors center and leads through a field where some bluebird boxes house both eastern bluebirds and tree swallows. Green darner dragonflies whirl past, and off in the Wildlife Habitat Demonstration Area are muskrat lodges. After passing the Goose Cove Picnic Area, the trail plunges into a wooded area that skirts the edge of the wildlife refuge. Deep-woods wildflowers such as rue anemone, common wood sorrel, and jack-in-the-pulpit live here, along with several fine shagbark hickory trees in a predominantly oak forest.

Rest on the bridge that crosses the middle branch of Chillisquaque Creek; then proceed between a pine and larch plantation on one side and a hayfield on the other until you reach Hickory Hollow Woods. Beyond that is a marsh at the edge of Jellyfish Cove, where, if you look closely, you might spot a wide variety of animal tracks in the mud or the probing holes made by the slanted, long bills of American woodcocks in search of earthworms.

Finally, proceed past the Heron Cove Picnic Area and back along the dam discharge area just below the visitors center. Then, if you are still not tired, cross the road to the self-guided Goose Woods Nature Trail, a portion of which is being developed for sight-impaired people, and take the three-quarter-mile walk along Chillisquaque Creek.

Because of the abundant waterfowl, spring and fall are the best times to visit the preserve, but a full day can be spent during any visit there. If you like formal programs, such as hikes led by professional naturalists or a variety of lectures, slide shows, and demonstrations by experts in their fields, write to Montour Preserve, R.D. 1, Box 292, Turbotville, PA 17772, or call 717-437-3131 and ask to be put on their quarterly-newsletter mailing list. Reservations for groups to use preserve facilities may also be made by calling the above number during office hours, from 9:00 A.M. until 4:00 P.M. Monday through Friday year-round. Visitors center hours on Saturday and Sunday are 2:00 P.M. until 5:00 P.M. from the second weekend in April to the second weekend in September. But the trails are open all year, and in winter cross-country skiing and ice fishing are popular.

From Williamsport: Follow U.S. Route 15 south 17 miles to the intersection of Interstate 80. Then take Interstate 80 east for 5 miles. Get off at Exit 32, Pa. 254, and turn left toward Limestoneville. Follow Route 254 east for 6.6 miles before turning left on Pa. 54 into Washingtonville. At the north end of Washingtonville (.4 mile further), turn right (sign points to power plant and preserve). After .9 mile turn left, still following preserve sign. Continue 2.6 miles straight past the power plant to the stop sign. Turn right. The entrance to the preserve is .5 mile further.

29 LOYALSOCK CREEK

The Loyalsock Creek area, in the Sullivan County Highlands, is a wonderful place to explore. It is already well known to trout fishermen and white-water rafting and canoeing enthusiasts, but anyone can enjoy its unique geologic formations, numerous hiking trails, several waterfalls, and outstanding canyon vista.

A short, easy hike to a section of the creek called the Haystacks provides an excellent introduction to the area. From the town of Laporte, where Route 220 intersects Route 154, proceed 2.8 miles further north on 220. On the left a sign for Loyalsock Trail marks the beginning of the fifty-nine-mile trail. Much of it is steep and rocky, but this portion follows an old, level railroad bed.

Park the car beside the highway and walk along Loyalsock Trail for about a mile. Much of the way will be through dense woods, and in late spring and summer the hemlock forest reverberates with the songs of breeding warblers and three melodious members of the thrush family—hermit thrushes, wood thrushes, and veeries. On the left the slope is a wild rock garden containing common wood sorrel, twinflowers, clintonia, starflowers, large white trillium, and Canada mayflowers. It is also a fernery, and common polypody, ostrich,

The Haystacks, Loyalsock Creek

interrupted, and hay-scented ferns are just a few of the species growing here.

About a thousand feet in from the trailhead, a hundred-yard detour on the right leads to Dutchman's Falls. An attractive, thirty-foot-high waterfall set in a dark, rocky hemlock grove, it is well worth the few minutes of effort to reach it.

After walking the mile along Loyalsock Trail, you will reach a prominent wooden sign labeled "The Haystacks ½ mile" and pointing to the right. The trail descends gently down toward the creek for a quarter mile before intersecting with trails coming in from both the left and right. Turn left and parallel Loyalsock Creek, following it downstream until you hear the shouts of children. You may also encounter backpack tents. Both the tents and the shouts are signals that you have reached the Haystacks.

Numerous large, rounded boulders, made of hard Burgoon sandstone, which is highly resistant to weather and water erosion, protrude several feet above the streambed. Between the rocks are small pools and short rapids. Since the water is shallow and only moderately fast, it is a favorite swimming hole for children. Pickerel frogs, American toads, and red eft salamanders represent a small sampling of the amphibians living along the moist stream-bank. Northern juncos are year-round residents and nest on rocky ledges beside the creek. Rose-breasted grosbeaks and red-eyed vireos are two of the seasonal bird visitors.

After walking back to your car, take another short ride to 275,000-acre World's End State Park on the Loyalsock Creek. Drive back to the intersection of Routes 220 and 154 and turn right. At 6.4 miles, shortly after crossing the park boundary, turn left at the sign marked "Loyalsock Canyon Vista 2 miles." Follow the excellent but narrow Mineral Spring dirt road for 1.4 miles. Then make a sharp left on Cold Run Road, which leads up to the vista on your left. After a long look down at the creek surrounded by the Allegheny Mountains, walk across the road and up a path that leads to the restrooms. Continue past them into an area called the Rock Garden on the park map.

This place also holds a strong attraction for children, but watch them carefully. Enormous rocks of a highly resistant, coarse-grained sandstone and conglomerate just beg to be climbed. However, frost action in the vertical rock joints has carved deep, narrow, interconnecting crevices in the boulders. These are fun to explore if you are surefooted, cautious, and reasonably slim, but the more sedate members of the group may prefer to examine the wide variety of moss, liverwort, and lichen species growing on the rocks or listen to bird songs. When we visited, we were treated to several calls from a barred owl at midday.

Return to Route 154 and drive another half mile to the entrance of Double Run Nature Trail on your left. This short spur follows along Double Run Stream, passing a small waterfall, for less than a half mile until it reaches a wooden bridge that crosses the stream. Unless you want to take a long, steep hike, turn back at this point.

In fact, save your desire to experience a steep, rocky trail until you drive another half mile to the main parking area. There you can park your car, reserve a picnic table, and then take the strenuous, mile-long High Rock Trail on the opposite side of the Loyalsock Creek. Follow the creek downstream until you reach a bridge, cross it, and immediately on the left you will see the yellow-blazed High Rock Trail and a warning sign about the trail's steepness.

At first I thought the sign was unnecessarily alarmist, because the climb up to High Rock Falls was gentle. But beyond that we clambered for several hundred feet up and over rocks painted with trail blazes. Eventually, with considerable muscle strain, we reached the top, where we had another view of the mountains and creek and saw more of the resistant sandstone outcrops. These rocks did not have quite the allure of the Rock Garden, and the view down was not as high as the Canyon Vista, but the fact that we had worked to reach them made them more satisfying. The descent is much easier, with a gentle slope and no rocks, and you quickly reach another bridge upstream, which you can cross back into the parking area and your car.

If you like High Rock Trail, there are many more steep, rocky trails in the park, including one up to the Canyon Vista. Facilities for family and organized-group camping, handicapped parking spaces and picnic areas, a small, dammed portion of the creek for swimming, white-water boating, trout fishing, hunting areas, and family cabins to rent make the Loyalsock Creek area an ideal choice for an outing.

From Williamsport: Take Route 220 east and then north to the town of Laporte (35 miles).

30 PINE CREEK GORGE

Pine Creek Gorge, often called the Grand Canyon of Pennsylvania, is the place to visit if you like views and a sense of brooding solitude. Two state parks, Leonard Harrison on the east rim and Colton Point on the west, offer numerous lookouts and short trails for people who want to explore this remote area in southern Tioga County.

Leonard Harrison is the first park to visit because it has a fine nature center and a short trail along the rim that gives an excellent introduction to the gorge, which was cut by glacial action thousands of years ago. Then, if you are at all agile, follow Turkey Path's descent one mile down to Pine Creek through a magnificent forest of hemlock and beech along Little Four Mile Run. A series of waterfalls three-quarters of a mile down the trail makes this walk particularly attractive. Part of this trail is also a nature trail that goes only halfway down and then returns. Ferns like the Christmas, marginal wood, bulblet, and maidenhair grow in the rocky ledges along the trail, and mosses and liverworts are prominent in the wet places. Bird song from such northern breeding species as red-breasted nuthatches, northern juncos, solitary vireos, northern waterthrushes, and Canada warblers can be heard in spring and early summer, while blue jays and black-capped chickadees dominate the late fall scene.

Once you reach the creek, you can explore along its edges, or, if the water is low, you can cross the creek and hike the steep mile and a half up Turkey Path through Colton Point Park. This is advisable only if one member of your party is willing to drive the car from one park to the other rather than hike the trail. Otherwise, retrace your steps to the rim at Leonard Harrison and drive back

Grand Canyon of Pennsylvania, Pine Creek Gorge

on Pa. Route 660 to Route 362, where you turn left and go to Ansonia.

At Ansonia take U.S. Route 6 west over the gorge and then turn left toward Colton Point State Park. Three miles along the road in the Tioga State Forest you will see a sign on the left for the Barbour Rock Nature Way Trail, an easy, one-mile circuit that leads through a young forest of hardwoods featuring both white and gray birch with an understory of striped maple, woodferns, several species of ground pine, and mountain laurel. About two hundred yards in along the blue-blazed trail, where the trail forks, continue slightly left until you reach the overlook. There you may see red-tailed hawks and turkey vultures circling overhead.

Turn right and follow orange blazes for a couple hundred feet along the rim until you reach the blue-blazed right turnoff back into the woods. This leads up a short incline and then down toward the trail fork again. Hermit thrushes, wood pewees, and chestnut-sided warblers, as well as a broad-winged hawk, were all in residence when we visited in mid-July. We also saw two white-tailed deer meandering across the little-used trail.

The Colton Point Park entrance is a further 1.4 miles by car. Fewer people visit this park, although it does have several road lookouts. At the parking lot three-tenths of a mile from the entrance, the orange-blazed Turkey Path Trail takes off on the right. This path is steeper, narrower, and longer (1.5 miles) on the west side of the gorge. Follow the trail past the intersection with West Rim Trail for about three hundred feet, where there is an active bee tree in a large white pine to the right of the trail.

Beyond this tree the path begins its precipitous hairpin, switchback descent to the bottom of the gorge. Along the way are a wide variety of wildflowers— columbine, jack-in-the-pulpit, wild ginger, false Solomon's seal, and Canada mayflowers in the spring, and the wild orchid helleborine, white snakeroot, hairy beardtongue, pointed-leaved tick trefoil, and red bee balm in the summer.

At the base of the gorge, just before you reach the creek, are several splendid cucumber trees. The banks of Pine Creek are lined with field flowers—daisies, coneflowers, joe-pye weed, Queen Anne's lace, teasel, bouncing bet, purple vervain, and tansy. People sun, wade, and fish here, and when the creek is high in the spring, white-water rafting is popular along stretches of the forty-mile-long gorge.

West Rim Trail is a rugged hike that backpackers can take, but for those who cannot manage even the steep Turkey Path, a short, circular walk in Colton Point Park over level terrain is an easy way to enjoy the area's beauty. Walk the short distance to the intersection of Turkey Path with West Rim Trail and turn right. This walk parallels the Rexford Branch stream for a half mile, leading through a forest of large white pines and hemlocks to the Colton dirt road. Turn right on the road and follow it back one-fifth of a mile to the park entrance road. Turn right again and then left onto Lookout Trail a hundred feet beyond park headquarters. Snyder Point View is the highlight of this walk. From here you can walk a short distance along the rim and then turn right back through a picnic area and the parking lot.

The most popular time to visit the Grand Canyon is in October when the autumn color is at its height, but if you are interested in birds and wildflowers, spring and summer are the best seasons. Fewer people are there then, and the trails are almost deserted. Picnicking and camping are allowed in each park, although Colton Point has more picnic facilities and covered pavilions, in addition to organized-group tenting and family camping. On the other hand, weekend programs and interpretive walks in the summertime take place only in Leonard Harrison State Park.

From Williamsport: Take U.S. Route 15 north 47 miles to Mansfield. Turn west onto U.S. Route 6 and drive 14 miles to Wellsboro. In Wellsboro take Route 660, which dead-ends in Leonard Harrison State Park.

31 FORREST H. DUTLINGER NATURAL AREA

The so-called Black Forest of Pennsylvania once covered a portion of eight northern counties with virgin hemlock trees so dense and thick "that the whole region had the appearance of a great black mass with scarcely an open spot to break the wonderful panorama of duskiness," as Judge Albert S. Heck declared in 1916. By then the entire area had been stripped of all its timber and had become "a million acres of desert in mid-Pennsylvania," as the chief of the U.S. Forest Service, Gifford Pinchot, described it.

But one 158-acre tract of virgin timber in northern Clinton County remained. Part of the Susquehannock State Forest, a 1,521-acre piece was set aside to protect this old-growth timber. First named Beech Bottom Hemlocks Natural Area by the Pennsylvania Bureau of Forestry, in 1979 it was renamed the Forrest H. Dutlinger Natural Area in honor of the then ninety-two-year-old resident of Huntingdon who in 1908 had been the first district forester to serve in the Renovo area.

Today it is not a place for the fainthearted. Although a four-wheel-drive vehicle can ford the Hammersley Fork creek, the mile-long "jeep road" is a real horror. It is best to park in the small lot on the east side of Hammersley Fork and cross over it on the well-constructed swinging footbridge. Then bear right for one mile on the "road" that parallels Hammersley Fork until it reaches Beech Bottom Run. Here Beech Bottom Run slips past several large, rounded boulders and cascades over a small but scenic waterfall before entering Hammersley Fork.

The trail, which is probably a former log slide, is on the left of Beech Bottom Run, and it follows steeply up the ravine for a mile through mostly second-growth hardwoods. Then, near the top, the hemlock trees become noticeably larger. This marks the old-growth stand, which also includes a scattering of white pine, red oak, American beech, sugar maple, and black gum trees. Experts theorize that only the virgin white pine was cut before a boundary dispute developed between two logging companies. Rather than risk illegal cutting, both companies abandoned the tract, leaving the virgin hemlocks and hardwoods as the sole monument to a once-vast forest.

The largest hemlock is on the left side of the trail; it measures 43 inches in diameter at breast-height and is 112 feet tall. Other hemlocks in the vicinity range from 32 to 40 inches in diameter. Except for an occasional croak from a pair of northern ravens and the faint sound of trickling water, the hollow is silent. On the steep banks Christmas ferns and woodferns are the predominant green ground cover, and red squirrels dash under boulders as soon as they see you coming.

Beech Bottom Run, Forrest H. Dutlinger Natural Area

The feeling of remoteness remains even when you find the trail register near the top of the trail filled with slips of paper left by others who have made the steep climb. They, too, mention the silence as the outstanding feature of the site.

Once you reach the top of the plateau, you can see where a blowdown in the early 1950s has allowed a variety of smaller trees to come up. Because a defined natural area must be maintained in a natural condition without human interference, large hemlocks that have fallen are not removed. A green covering of thick fern moss grows on them and serves as a fertile starter for dozens of hemlock seedlings. Trees like these are called nurse trees.

Other large trees in the area are black cherry, basswood, white ash, red maple, black birch, white oak, and chestnut oak, but foresters believe these species grew up only after the virgin white pine was cut.

Beech Bottom Run eventually trickles out on the plateau, marked by several boggy areas with sphagnum moss. Woodpeckers are plentiful, particularly hairy woodpeckers. Northern juncos are common in the autumn, and the fallen logs along the stream attract winter wrens. Black bears, wild turkeys, and white-tailed deer also use the area.

Beech Bottom Trail is well defined for several hundred feet over the plateau, but then it peters out, so it is best to retrace your steps down the hollow.

Because the trail is steep, you should be in moderately good shape to attempt it, and a cool fall day is probably the best time to visit. Judging from the trail register, the area attracts mostly young adults, but I found I needed only one stop to pant my way to the top. It is well worth the effort to make the climb so you can see what the Black Forest of Pennsylvania looked like before the lumbermen did their work.

From Williamsport: Take Route 220 west to Lock Haven. At Lock Haven turn north onto Pa. Route 120 toward Renovo. Drive through Renovo on 120 until you reach Pa. Route 144 north. Follow 144 approximately 10 miles to the broad bridge over Kettle Creek. At 1.6 miles north of Kettle Creek Bridge, take the unnamed road to the left. After one-tenth of a mile, turn left again on a dirt road immediately beyond a bridge over Hammersley Fork. Proceed .5 mile on the dirt road until you reach the Hammersley Fork Run ford. Park on the right above the creek.

32 BUCKTAIL STATE PARK

Bucktail State Park stretches for seventy-five miles along the Susquehanna River and Sinnemahoning Creek from Lock Haven northwest to Emporium. Billed as Pennsylvania's largest natural area (16,328 acres), in reality it is a thin strip of land running between mountain ridges, with a well-paved, scenic road for those who enjoy viewing the outdoors from car windows. In addition, there

View from Hyner Run Vista, Bucktail State Park

are many miles of hiking trails in the two state forests, five state parks, four wild areas, and six natural areas that surround Bucktail State Park.

For a day that combines great views and a couple of easy walks in natural areas, start at Lock Haven and take Route 120 west for 20 miles. Turn right at a sign for Hyner Run State Park and Hyner Run Vista. After 1.7 miles another sign directs you to a sharp right toward the vista, which is 2.6 miles along a narrow, winding macadam road.

At the top are a picnic grove, stone memorials to former state foresters, and one of the best views in the state. On a crystal-clear day in early autumn, it is particularly spectacular since Hyner Run Vista is 1,940 feet above sea level and the mountain drops 1,300 feet to the river below.

After your introductory view of the area, retrace your way to Route 120 west and continue northwest for six miles to Renovo. Then turn left on Route 144 south and drive 9.1 miles, slowly ascending through woods until you reach the mountaintop and a large blowdown, one of the many areas destroyed by tornadoes in May 1985. Turn left onto Beech Creek Road and proceed .7 mile to an unmarked dirt road. Then make a right and drive a half mile to the yellow-blazed East Branch Trail on the right. From here it is an easy one-eighth of a mile in to the East Branch Swamp Natural Area, a 186-acre reconstituted bog that was created when the water table was altered after a logging operation.

Today it is a quiet, remote spot with a few weathered stumps still sticking above the lowbush blueberries, sphagnum moss, cattail swales, rushes, and sedges that thrive in the wet meadow. A large, flat rock makes an excellent seat from which to observe the butterflies, dragonflies, and birds flying over the bog. Along the swamp margin grows a mixed stand of oak and twenty acres of virgin hemlocks. Although it is difficult to believe, the bog is actually forty feet higher (1,980 feet) than Hyner Run Vista.

After enjoying the peace and beauty of a mountaintop bog, return to your car and drive back to Renovo. Halfway along the paved road on your right is the Jesse Hall State Forest Picnic Area, an excellent place to enjoy a packed lunch.

In the center of Renovo, turn left again onto Pa. Route 120 west and drive 23.8 miles to where a bridge crosses left over Sinnemahoning Creek. After the crossing follow Wykoff Run Road 9.7 miles until it meets the Quehanna Highway. Here you can park and take the blue-blazed Quehanna Cross-Country Ski Trail, which leads back to the right through the heart of the Wykoff Run Natural Area.

Wykoff Run Natural Area, 245 acres in the center of the Quehanna Wild Area, is best known for its large, beautiful stand of paper birch trees, which gives the woods a northern New England look. There are also several imposing hemlocks scattered amid the red maple–mixed oak forest with its heavy ground cover of ferns. White-tailed deer, gray squirrels, eastern chipmunks, and red-tailed hawks are just a sampling of the wildlife you may see in this protected area.

The open meadow around a long-abandoned farm site also has a more northerly aspect because of the purple, composite steeplebush that grows there in abundance. In late summer the meadow supports numerous hooded ladies' tresses—a wild orchid—pearly everlasting, white snakeroot, and several species of goldenrod. Trailing arbutus is the featured wildflower attraction in early spring.

It is best to return the way you came on the cross-country ski trail when you reach the dirt road that forms the northeast boundary of Wykoff Run Natural Area. Then, depending on where you live, you can either retrace your route to Lock Haven or take the Quehanna Highway south to the Karthaus area and turn right on 879 toward Clearfield for Interstate 80 west or left toward Snowshoe for Interstate 80 east.

For autumn color and the clearest views, early October is the best time to visit. But if cross-country skiing is your sport, the Quehanna Cross-Country Ski Trail is certainly worth a winter visit. For those who don't wish or are unable to hike, a drive down the entire length of Bucktail State Park from Lock Haven to Emporium and back again will give you a scenic overview of some of the wildest country in Pennsylvania.

From Lock Haven: Take Route 120 west for 20 miles.

33 BEAR MEADOWS NATURAL AREA

Bear Meadows Natural Area is a 520-acre boreal sphagnum bog sixty miles southwest of the nearest glaciation that occurred during the last Ice Age. Located in the ridge-and-valley section of central Pennsylvania seven miles south of State College, this National Natural Landmark is surrounded by mountain ridges 400 to 600 feet higher than the bog. The bog itself is 1,820 feet above sea level, more than twice as high as the Tannersville Bog in the Poconos.

It is unusual to find a boreal bog so far south of the glaciated region, and many boreal plants and trees more commonly found in the floating bogs of Canada and the Poconos—such as leatherleaf, bog laurel, balsam fir, and black spruce—thrive at Bear Meadows. The carnivorous round-leaved sundew as well as wild orchids—the round-leaved orchis, yellow-fringed orchis, and heartleaf twayblade—also grow here, as do corn lily, goldthread, starflower, highbush blueberry, and several species of sedges, rushes, and wild grasses. Unfortunately, excessive collecting has destroyed the pitcher-plant population.

Ten thousand years ago there was a pond at Bear Meadows, but either a beaver dam or a landslide blocked the outlet to Sinking Creek. Over the

Berry-pickers on the observation platform, Bear Meadows Natural Area

centuries the area gradually filled in with sphagnum moss, which formed a seven-foot-deep peat layer beneath it. Today Sinking Creek drains the bog, leaving only a one-and-a-quarter-mile strip of open bog. This is gradually being invaded by the surrounding forest of black spruce, red maple, black gum, hemlock, and balsam fir, along with a dense stand of rhododendron. Although recent beaver activity over two seasons raised the water level (which is now gradually receding), there is some fear that the plant population may have been permanently altered.

In addition to the black bears that come to feast on blueberries, and the hordes of hipboot-clad, bucket-carrying humans, white-tailed deer and eastern chipmunks are the other common mammals. Sixteen species of warblers, including the more northerly Canada, hooded, and parula warblers, nest here, and over a thirty-five-year period entomologists have identified fifty-eight species of dragonflies.

To visit Bear Meadows on a clear, bright summer day when the blueberries are ripe and the mosquitoes are sluggish is a rare treat. Park in the lot beside the bridge over Sinking Creek and slip down beside the creek to watch the dragonflies. Then cross the road and examine the arrow-leaved pondweed in bloom before following the short path on the parking-lot side of the road through the woods to the observation platform. Built in 1978 by Centre County's CETA (Comprehensive Employment and Training Act) workers, it gives you a good view of the surrounding bog and mountain ridges. From here you may spot such birds as cedar waxwings, white-throated sparrows, American goldfinches, least flycatchers, gray catbirds, red-eyed vireos, and black-capped chickadees.

Just in case you get tired of wading in the sometimes waist-high, peat-stained, acidic water in search of blueberries, there is an easy, 3.5-mile, level hiking trail through the oak-hardwood forest just beyond the bog. From the observation platform walk straight through the rhododendron–hemlock–white pine woods until you reach an obvious jeep trail. The trail is rocky in places with wet spots, but later it becomes dry and grassy. Turn right and walk for about a mile until you pass a blue-blazed trail on your left; this will merge into the jeep trail for about a quarter of a mile before it turns back off to the left again. Continue ahead on the unblazed trail, with the bog always on your right.

After crossing a footbridge, you emerge into a meadowlike opening. Turn right and follow a good packed-dirt road for 1.4 miles along the north side of the bog. Then you will come to North Meadows Road, where you turn right and walk another .2 mile before reaching Bear Meadows Road. Continue right a further .6 mile to complete the circular hike. An alternative is to turn right on a blue-blazed trail just before you reach Bear Meadows Road; this trail also leads back to the parking area.

Although the bog itself may be packed with berry pickers, the hiking trail may be deserted, and you are more likely to catch glimpses of the area's abundant wildlife. Spend some time in the rhododendron–hemlock–white pine belt between the bog and the hardwoods. If the season has been wet, you may find interesting fungi like the black dead-man's-fingers (*Xylosphaera poly-morpha*), which are club-shaped or fingerlike, and the yellow *Clavariadelphus ligula,* also cylindrical but more narrowly club-shaped or flattened. Both grow in clumps under coniferous trees.

Mid-July to early August is the best time to visit if blueberry picking is your highest priority, but by then the rhododendron blossoms will have dropped. To see them at their height early July is best. However, autumn, when the highbush blueberry leaves turn wine-red and American goldfinches sing as they dip over the bog, is also lovely.

From State College: Follow Route 322 east to Boalsburg. From the traffic light at

Boalsburg continue straight through on Route 322 for 1.9 miles. Turn right on a road with a sign for Tussey Mountain Ski Resort. After .6 mile, swing right on the main road and continue .8 mile until you reach Bear Meadows Road to the left. Follow Bear Meadows Road straight ahead for 3.5 miles, where you take the right fork another .1 mile. The parking lot will be on your right.

34 ALAN SEEGER NATURAL AREA

The Alan Seeger Natural Area in Huntingdon County has one of the best examples of a virgin hemlock stand in the state. Although the largest giant fell during a storm in May 1982, another hemlock, almost as impressive, is estimated to be more than five hundred years old.

While much of the rest of the surrounding forest was being burned for charcoal, this 118-acre remnant was spared. Botanist E. Lucy Braun, in her book *Deciduous Forest of Eastern North America,* called it a perfect example of a hemlock-forest type of ravine, a dense, almost pure hemlock-rhododendron community that "occupies a broad, flat-bottomed ravine in which the stream is but slightly entrenched." Along with hemlock and rhododendron, white oak and red maple are the abundant species, and because the trees are so large the smaller plants are sparse.

It is to see the giant hemlocks and interlocking canopy of twenty-foot-high rhododendrons growing along the three-quarter-mile circular Alan Seeger Trail that most people visit the area. Wildly racing Detweiler Run and Stone Creek also attract trout fishermen. The forest's dense coolness on a hot summer day during the first week of July is an added benefit for visitors coming to see the magnificent rhododendron stand in full bloom.

From the parking lot, walk along Stone Creek Road for a hundred feet until you reach a large signboard with a map of the area. This is where the Alan Seeger Trail begins. Follow the trail as it winds through meadowlike growth beneath magnificent, large white oaks and red maples, several small white pines, a shagbark hickory, and a scattering of other hardwoods. Some of the trees are identified with labels. Black-capped chickadees and chipping sparrows are common in this section, and in spring trout lilies, Canada mayflowers, pink lady's slippers, fringed polygala, and sweet white violets punctuate the forest floor. Under the rhododendrons in June and July you may be able to find Small's twayblade, a southern wild orchid that grows only in a few places in Pennsylvania.

Once you turn right and cross the bridge, you are plunged into a dense

Greenwood Spur–Johnson Trail, Alan Seeger Natural Area

growth of rhododendrons and hemlocks that inspires silence. Only a red-eyed vireo broke the peace during one of my visits in midsummer. Otherwise I wandered transfixed from hemlock to hemlock, craning my neck to look up at the giant of them all—112 feet high and thick enough for three people to join hands around. There is also a sizable tulip tree and several large white pines.

Cross a footbridge over Stone Creek and then bear right through more open woods until you reach Seeger Road. Turn right and walk a short distance to the unmarked Mill Race Trail, which parallels Stone Creek for less than a tenth of a mile. A fallen five-hundred-year-old hemlock, the remains of an old millrace, the beauty of the rushing Stone Creek and the tiny pools filled with several species of attractive mosses, including a sphagnum, make this a charming if poorly defined trail.

Retrace your steps to the road and turn left again until you reach, on the right side of the road just before the Alan Seeger Trail exit, the blue-blazed Greenwood Spur–Johnson Trail. Cross a double log bridge over the stream and follow the trail up the mountain for true solitude. The trail begins in a hemlock forest and climbs gently up into a hardwood zone. Several open beds of hay-scented ferns gleam golden in the sunlight of a summer's day. Off to the right a woodland pond can be cautiously circled. Wood frogs, cattails, sedges, jack-in-the-pulpits, wolf's-claw club moss, several species of violets, Indian pipes, and sensitive, maidenhair, rattlesnake, and polypody ferns thrive beside the pond. Wood pewees and rufous-sided towhees sing and call.

Three hundred yards beyond the pond, where a hollow begins to form on your left, take a left onto an unmarked woods road. Cross a small mountain stream and proceed a mile back to Seeger Road. Finally, turn left and walk along the road to Alan Seeger Natural Area.

Because of the blooming rhododendron and Small's twayblade, early July is the best time to visit, but spring is the season to enjoy the ephemeral wild-flowers, and deep winter has its charms for snowshoers and cross-country skiers.

Since the trails are easy and relatively short, this is an excellent place to take older people, although groups of all ages would enjoy the Alan Seeger Natural Area. If you take a Scout troop or other young people, there are a number of longer, more challenging trails in the area that could extend your day. Picnic tables and covered pavilions are also available to accommodate visitors.

From State College: Follow Route 26 south to Pine Grove Mills. Turn left at the blinker light on Route 26 over Tussey Mountain. Proceed 9.2 miles to McAlevy's Fort. Look for a sharp left turn onto a paved road just after passing signs for McAlevy's Fort. Once you turn you will see a sign on your left saying "Alan Seeger Monument 8 miles." At .8 mile turn right. A further 1.9 miles and the paved road makes a sharp left; continue .1 mile to a sharp right, where there is a sign to Alan Seeger and the paved road becomes gravel. At 2.2 miles the road again is paved at the entrance to state forest land. Continue following the road 1.2 miles and then turn right into a parking lot at Alan Seeger Natural Area.

35 THE BARRENS

The Barrens, four miles southwest of State College in Centre County, typifies a unique habitat fast disappearing from the eastern United States. Also known as State Game Lands 176, this area was first referred to as a barrens by the Shawnee Indians because of its infertile, acidic, sand-and-clay soil. Yet the Indians claimed that huge trees and outsized animals lived in the area until the nineteenth century, when Andrew Carnegie developed an iron-ore mine there.

Scotia Pond, the Barrens

Subsequent logging and repeated burning reduced the Barrens to the scrub oak–blueberry community that persists today. But its sandy soil with low water-holding capacity hosts a number of wild plants and creatures rare in Pennsylvania, including buck moths, hognose snakes, and wildflowers like the hoary puccoon and wild lupine. Pine barrens are endangered, along with the unique creatures that live in them. The Barrens, with its ten-thousand-acre, three-tiered, savannalike growth, is the largest barren left in Pennsylvania and the fifth largest in the eastern United States.

Another unusual feature of the Barrens is its penetrating cold. Freezing temperatures are liable to occur here at any time of the year because the combination of small, scrubby vegetation and sandy soil creates what scientists call an "active radiation surface," in which the ground deflects the heat and absorbs the cold. Temperatures as low as forty degrees below zero have been recorded here in winter, but at any time it may be as much as thirty degrees colder than nearby State College, so visitors are advised to wear warmer clothes here no matter what the season.

Most visitors' favorite destination is Scotia Pond, which is rimmed with buttonbush and meadowsweet and reverberates with the deep croaks of bullfrogs. Dragonflies and damselflies zoom past, while great blue and green-backed herons can often be spotted in the shallows.

As you pick your way along an ill-defined and sometimes moist trail that circles the water, common yellowthroats, song sparrows, and northern orioles sing. If you are lucky you may spot a Fowler's toad—an abundant species on the Atlantic Coastal Plain, but found only in sandy soil further inland—or a common water snake. In the woods the ground is carpeted in places with the attractive leaves of spotted wintergreen.

After exploring the pond, return to your car and drive a further .2 mile to a road on the right that leads to the clay pits near the site of the former Scotia iron mines. Unfortunately, target shooters frequently use this area, so be sure to make a lot of noise as you approach. The clay pits attract at least five species of tiger beetles. The attractive, red, iron-impregnated rocks are another drawing card, and in late spring lance-leaved violets bloom beside the pools of water at the base of the pit.

From the clay pits you can continue by car along the main dirt road through the game lands, scanning the roadside for such lovely wildflowers as wood betony, wild lupines, and hoary puccoons. Or you can stop whenever you see an intriguing trail. It was off one such trail, on barren, sandy hillocks, that we found a hognose snake on two different visits. Each time it flattened out its head like a cobra, puffed itself up like an adder, and hissed intimidatingly. This harmless snake, with its upturned nose, mottled, light-colored belly, and patterned back, never bites when it is threatened. Instead it either does its cobra-adder act or it opens its mouth, shudders, rolls over on its back, and plays dead.

A little more than two miles beyond Scotia Pond you will come to the official target range as well as a few picnic tables and indoor facilities with restrooms and a water fountain. You might also find Game Commission personnel here who can fill you in on the current research being done at the Barrens on such game animals as ruffed grouse, white-tailed deer, cottontail rabbits, and wild turkeys, all of which are abundant here.

It is best to visit during cool spring and summer days or even in the winter, when cross-country skiing is popular. Once hunting season begins, you should go there only on Sundays. However, if you want to see one of the rarest moths in the eastern United States, you must explore the scrub-oak areas of the Barrens in the fall from mid-morning to mid-afternoon, when the buck moths are flying. Named "buck moth" because their appearance coincides with deer-hunting season, these attractive black moths with white wing bands and red markings can live only in pine barrens that support a good population of scrub or bear oaks. Current research indicates that they are now found in fourteen of the twenty-two barren areas in the East. Because barren habitats are subject to wildfires—common usually from February through May—these moths evolved as a fall-reproducing species.

On the other hand, tiger beetles and hognose snakes are easier to find in warm summer weather, while the unusual wildflowers are at their height in late May and throughout June. So visit here frequently to get the full flavor of this endangered habitat, secure in the knowledge that because the Barrens is largely owned by the Game Commission it will not be sacrificed for housing tracts, the fate of most of the once-vast pine barrens in the eastern United States.

From downtown State College: Follow North Atherton Street (Route 322 west) 4.4 miles to the intersection with Scotia Road (.2 mile from the Mt. Nittany Expressway). Turn left and follow Scotia Road .9 mile. Turn left again on the second road to the left and drive .4 mile to Scotia Pond on the left.

36 TROUGH CREEK STATE PARK

Trough Creek State Park in Huntingdon County is part of the ridge-and-valley province of the Appalachian Mountains. Over eons, Trough Creek has cut down through sandstone and conglomerate rock to form a long, narrow valley, part of which was flooded by nearby Raystown Dam in 1975.

Today the park has 541 acres of mountains and creek bottomlands with cliffs, waterfalls, and three interesting geologic features: an ice mine, Balanced Rock, and Copperas Rock. The surrounding forest is composed of hemlocks and northern hardwoods in the creek bottomlands, with a predominantly mixed-oak community higher up on the mountains.

It is the three unusual geologic features that make the park unique. Geologists call Balanced Rock an "erosion remnant," which simply means that it was left behind when Trough Creek cut its valley millions of years ago. It is made of sandstone that broke away from rock cliffs that have since crumbled away. Over long stretches of geologic time, this particular rock moved slowly downhill as other rock blocks below it weathered away. Finally, it stopped at the edge of a cliff, where it hangs today. Copperas Rock is a colorful, massive outcropping still being undercut by Trough Creek. Someday it too may become a "balanced" rock.

While both Copperas Rock and Balanced Rock are natural geologic fea-

Balanced Rock, Trough Creek State Park

tures, the ice mine had some help from man. An opening was dug into the
mountain, possibly as a prospect hole, during mining days. In late spring and
early summer ice builds up at the mine entrance because the warm, moist air
of the outside is colliding with the cold winter air that had been trapped in the
crumbled rock mass on the mountain above.

The best way to see Copperas Rock and Balanced Rock is to park at the
Copperas Rock picnic ground and spend some time walking along the creek
and studying the imposing cliffs, which include Copperas Rock itself. Then
walk across the road to Copperas Rock Trail, which, strangely enough, does
not go past the rock at all but heads in the opposite direction. After walking a
hundred yards, turn right on Rhododendron Trail, the nicest trail in the park.
Most of the way it follows above Trough Creek through a thick growth of
rhododendron and hemlocks.

There is a short ascent on Abbot Run Trail to Balanced Rock, which,
unfortunately, is covered with painted names and initials; nevertheless, its size
and seemingly precarious balance are impressive. However, it has hung here

for thousands of years and will probably continue to do so for many thousand more.

To see the ice mine, descend Abbot Run Trail to Rhododendron Trail. Turn right and proceed about 600 feet until you reach a suspension bridge. Cross it and take a short path up to the main park road. Then walk a half mile back to your car at Copperas Rock. Drive out to the end of the park road, leave the car in a parking lot, and descend the covered stairs to the opening of the ice mine.

After seeing the ice and feeling the blast of cold air, you may want to walk another interesting trail. Lakeside Trail, just beyond the ice mine where the road is barricaded, is a part of the old park road. This trail parallels man-made Raystown Lake for a half mile, and in the years since dam water filled in this portion of the valley, the road has been overtaken by natural forces. It is cracked and heaved in many places, and Virginia creeper vines sprawl across the crumbling macadam. Finally, the road disappears into the water.

The best time to visit the park is in late spring or early summer if you are interested in seeing the ice mine. In addition, Abbot Run Trail follows along a part of Trough Creek that includes several cascades and waterfalls best seen during the high-water period in spring. However, late summer and fall are also good times to go, especially if you are interested primarily in hiking and camping.

Trough Creek has more than three hundred picnic tables, thirty tent and trailer sites, and sixteen miles of trails. Since the park is adjacent to Rothrock State Forest and Raystown Lake, a whole weekend could be spent comparing the man-made environment of Raystown Lake to the valley formed by the slow forces of nature.

From Altoona: Follow Route 36 (Logan Boulevard) south through Hollidaysburg. Continue south on 36 for 8 miles to its junction with Route 164 near Roaring Spring. Turn left on 164, go 4 miles into Martinsburg, and continue 6 more miles on Route 164 east to junction of Pa. Route 26. Turn left on 26. Go 6 miles to junction with Route 994 at Entriken. Turn right on 994. Go through Entriken and continue on across Raystown Lake. At 5.3 miles from Route 26, turn left onto plainly marked entrance road into park. At 1.8 miles turn left again; Copperas Rock parking lot is a further 1.4 miles. Continue along the same road another 1.2 miles to the ice mine and Lakeside Trail.

37 LITTLE JUNIATA WATER GAP NATURAL AREA

A water gap is caused by a river carving a course through a mountain ridge. Such gaps are common in the ridge-and-valley province of the Appalachian Mountains, and because they make ideal routes for roads, very few of the scenic water gaps in Pennsylvania are without highways. The Little Juniata Water Gap in Huntingdon County is one of them. And here a prime trout-fishing area as well as a natural area has been established.

Although hikers and fishermen will not hear the noise of cars and trucks as they pursue their peaceful hobbies, they will often hear the whistle of trains since the main line of the east-west railroad goes through part of the gap before entering a tunnel at the northern end of Short Mountain.

The Pennsylvania Fish Commission maintains a parking lot at the entrance to the natural area, where two trails begin. One leads partway through the gap, and the other straight up Tussey Mountain. Both are part of the orange-blazed Mid-State Trail.

While you are still fresh, take the steep trail that climbs from 700 to 1,600 feet above sea level in a little over a mile. The beginning is the steepest, rockiest part of the walk, but soon the rocks are interspersed with a green bed of moss and the trail's incline becomes gentler. A steady, slow pace up to the first view at a little over 1,400 feet should be possible for most people in reasonable physical condition.

The views, which are all to the left of the trail, are what make the effort worthwhile. A boulder outcropping covered with crusty toadskin lichens marks the first overlook. From here you can sit almost at eye level with the birds of prey that use the gap as a highway during migration, and through the trees you can glimpse the shine of the rails below.

A short climb a couple hundred feet further brings the hiker to a level shelf and the remains of what was once a quarry where Tuscarora sandstone was dug out to use as a lining in charcoal iron furnaces and as railroad ballast. Now it is overgrown with shrubs and trees.

The trail keeps to the left and becomes grassy. From open rockslides you can look out over the gap and a lovely series of ridges and small valleys. After several hundred feet the orange blazes lead sharply right up a much steeper grade, but you should continue straight for a short distance on the level, narrow path to get a further short series of views before turning back and retracing your steps to the parking lot.

After seeing the Little Juniata Water Gap from the heights, it is time to explore its depths. Follow the dirt road that begins at the north end of the parking lot and runs above the river and railroad tracks. The trail climbs a

Overlook, Little Juniata Water Gap

gentle grade, and for a while you can hear but not see the river. The constant variety of wildflowers growing on and beside the trail—several species of goldenrods, white wood asters, starry campion, and white snakeroot in late summer and early autumn—makes this section of the trail interesting.

Walk eight-tenths of a mile on the orange-blazed trail. Then watch carefully on your left for a double orange blaze leading down over a railroad bridge. Do not take that trail. Instead follow the wider, unmarked trail slightly to the right and straight into the gap. Almost immediately the trail dips down next to the river, and on the right large cliffs enclose the narrow area. The trail is sometimes faint, but there is no way you can get lost since the river is on your left and the mountain on your right.

This is the heart of the Little Juniata Water Gap—a peaceful place where only the rattling calls of belted kingfishers or the loud hammering of pileated woodpeckers interrupt the quiet. Even the train whistles are muffled as the trains disappear into the tunnel. Along the riverside in the mud are the hoofprints of white-tailed deer; and, depending on the season, such wild-flowers as violets, jack-in-the-pulpit, columbine, Solomon's seal, joe-pye weed, coneflowers, silverrod, and sneezeweeds grow on the riverbank.

The two most impressive features of the gap are the increasingly imposing rock outcroppings, some with overhanging shelves, and the many large, possibly virgin, oaks growing beside the river. Other fine trees include red maple, black willow, sycamore, tulip, and striped maple. About a half mile along the unmarked trail is a beautiful hemlock grove with a couple of massive white and red oaks. A rock cairn has been built up in the middle of the grove with a roughly made wooden cross stuck in the top. Several logs have been arranged as benches, and there are the remains of campfires. This is the loveliest place in the natural area, remote and peaceful, an ideal location for eating lunch, resting, and contemplating the majesty of the trees and the pristine river below.

From here you can continue to pick your way along the river for another half mile until you reach an old hunting camp on the right. This marks the end of the natural area and the beginning of private land, so you must turn around and retrace your steps for the two miles back to the parking lot.

Early autumn is the best time to visit the Little Juniata Water Gap Natural Area. The wildflowers are varied and lovely then; the migrating birds of prey, like the osprey we saw close up at the first lookout, are flying through; and the views are more likely to be crystal-clear.

The crude wayside shrine indicates that the gap is popular with church groups. Our local Juniata Valley Audubon Society has also hiked here in October. In fact, the Little Juniata Water Gap Natural Area makes a lovely outing any time for hikers, trout fishermen, tree-lovers, wildflower fanciers, and bird watchers.

From Altoona: Take Frankstown Road over Brush Mountain about 4 miles. At the stop sign on U.S. 22 turn left on Route 22 east. Proceed 16 miles to Water Street, the junction of Pa. 453 and 22. Continue east on 22 for .5 mile. Turn left into Alexandria. At 1.2 miles turn left immediately past the Mead Products factory. Follow the country road less than 2 miles through the village of Barree. Make a sharp left on the bridge over the Little Juniata River. Several hundred feet beyond the bridge, turn left onto Porter Township Road 514. Follow the road up the river .6 mile to the parking area just beyond the end of the pavement.

38 TYTOONA NATURAL AREA

The Tytoona Natural Area, in bucolic Sinking Valley near Altoona, has the only cave in the state that has been preserved as a natural area. Owned and administered by the Western Pennsylvania Conservancy, Tytoona Cave is of international significance because of its unique "soda straw" formations.

The 6.8 acres purchased by the Conservancy contain the cave entrance, steep limestone cliffs, and a surrounding wooded area. The cave is tucked away at the base of the cliffs, which have enough soil to support a fine growth of hemlock trees near the top. Dainty, ledge-loving maidenhair spleenwort ferns grow near the bottom.

Liverworts, moss, and bright orange lichens thrive on the wet rocks lining the stream that gushes out from beneath a cliff and thunders back into the cave. Tytoona Cave itself is, according to Dr. William White of Penn State, a "window into an underground drainage system." Unlike most Pennsylvania caves, Tytoona Cave contains a large underground stream that floods the cave's inner chambers and the connecting passages, thus making most of the cave exceedingly dangerous to explore.

Paradoxically, with its 40-foot-wide, twelve-foot-high opening, it is also one of the easiest caves to enter in central Pennsylvania. Using only a flashlight (or, better yet, two, in case one burns out and leaves you in total darkness), you can follow a well-defined trail for several hundred feet and feel the droplets of water seeping from the cave roof.

Water seeping through limestone rock has formed both stalactites (hanging from the ceiling) and stalagmites (rising from the cave floor). Those formations in the outer chamber of Tytoona Cave were destroyed long ago by vandalism and strong water and air currents. But those in the water-filled rooms beyond—two of which were discovered by cave divers in the 1960s and a further room reached in the summer of 1985—are unique "soda straw" formations, or hollow stalactites fourteen to sixteen feet long. These rare, pencil-thin tubes, developed over the last 25,000 years, are clear white and highly crystalline. Only in an Australian cave have similar formations been found.

The average person will never see these stalactites since only people trained in the sport of cave diving can reach the inner chambers. But you can follow a short, steep trail down to the entrance of the cave, admire the cliffs, and walk a short way into the cave with your flashlight. Then spend some time, if it is spring, searching for the ephemeral wildflowers—jack-in-the-pulpit, hepatica, rue anemone, bloodroot, Dutchman's-breeches, wild ginger, cut-leaved tooth-wort, bishop's cap, and smooth yellow violets—that grow in the adjoining woodland.

Cave entrance, Tytoona Natural Area

Finally, you can explore Sinking Valley itself, a beautiful farm valley. Stop and visit the reconstructed, Revolutionary War–era Fort Roberdeau, formerly called Lead Mine Fort. It is open free to the public from the beginning of May until the end of September, and costumed guides lead tours through the buildings from 11:00 A.M. until 5:00 P.M. every day except Monday. Groups can also be accommodated then (or even in April and October) if you call ahead (814-946-0048) and ask for the director.

If you want to eat a picnic lunch or explore well-maintained trails that meander through twenty-nine acres of unspoiled woodlands, stop at the Fort Roberdeau Nature Center, directly across from the fort area, any time of the year from dawn until dusk.

From Altoona: Follow Kettle Road over Brush Mountain, past the Kettle Reservoir and into Sinking Valley. Pass the entrance to Fort Roberdeau on the left 8 miles from the Pleasant Valley Boulevard (Route 220) intersection. Proceed straight another 3.5 miles (11.9 miles from Route 220) and turn left on an unmarked gravel road. The cave entrance is .3 mile up the road on the left. If you pass the Sinking Valley Presbyterian Church on the right on the main valley road, you have gone too far. Turn around and go back 1.1 miles to the gravel road.

WESTERN PENNSYLVANIA

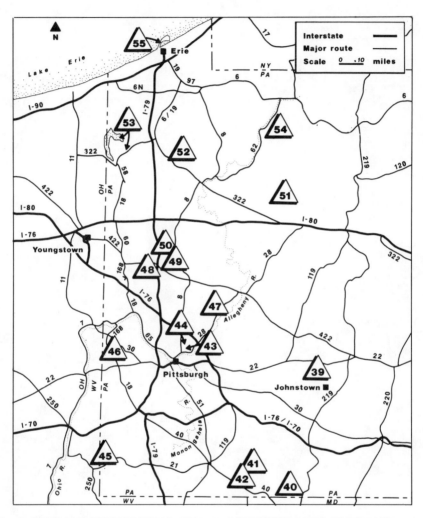

39. CHARLES F. LEWIS NATURAL AREA
40. MT. DAVIS NATURAL AREA
41. FALLINGWATER
42. OHIOPYLE STATE PARK
43. TRILLIUM TRAIL
44. BEECHWOOD FARMS NATURE
    RESERVE
45. ENLOW FORK NATURAL AREA
46. RACCOON CREEK STATE PARK
47. TODD SANCTUARY

48. MCCONNELLS MILL STATE PARK
49. JENNINGS ENVIRONMENTAL
    EDUCATION CENTER
50. WOLF CREEK NARROWS NATURAL
    AREA
51. COOK FOREST STATE PARK
52. ERIE NATIONAL WILDLIFE REFUGE
53. PYMATUNING LAKE
54. ALLEGHENY NATIONAL FOREST
55. PRESQUE ISLE STATE PARK

39 CHARLES F. LEWIS NATURAL AREA

The Charles F. Lewis Natural Area near Johnstown is a 384-acre tract of mountain land on Laurel Ridge that includes a rushing stream with several small waterfalls, many of the showier ephemeral wildflower species, and a large jumble of enormous boulders and overhanging ledges. Its only facilities are two picnic tables near the parking lot, which you can use either before or after you take the mildly strenuous Clark Run Trail for its three-mile circuit through the natural area. Better yet, carry along a lunch so you can walk slowly and spend the day in this peaceful place where the rushing water blots out all other sounds except for the loud, ringing calls of Louisiana water-thrushes in the spring.

Spring, when it is still cool, the stream is high, and the mountainside is a wildflower garden, is definitely the season to take Clark Run Trail. The most difficult parts of the trail are the fairly steep climb near the beginning, the gentle descent through the boulder area, and a steep descent at the end, but any moderately fit person should be able to make it with good hiking shoes.

Walk under the gateway and into the woods, taking the clearly marked, orange-blazed Clark Run Trail as it turns right up a short flight of stairs. From here until you reach a woods road the trail parallels the stream.

The largest waterfall is close to the bottom of the mountain, so it is possible to walk in just to see the long, narrow shoot of water hemmed in by huge boulders and framed by stately rhododendron bushes. Along the lower banks of Clark Run, Canada mayflowers, round-leaved yellow violets, and white trillium bloom in April and May, but as you ascend the trail you can look for wild ginger on the left and a hillside of both large white and purple or red trillium on the right. Large American beech trees are another feature of this section of the natural area.

After the trail levels out and just before it reaches the old woods road, where you turn left, beds of mayapples, trout lilies, cut-leaved toothworts, and blue cohosh grow near the stream, and a small waterfall sheets thinly over a series of low moss-covered ledges. This is an idyllic spot to rest before con-

Rock formations, Charles F. Lewis Natural Area

tinuing on up the road until you come to an open meadow that covers the remains of an old charcoal hearth.

Turn left on a wooden bridge over Clark Run and continue to follow the old woods road until you see a black-and-yellow steel gate ahead. Approximately a hundred feet before the gate the orange blazes bear left. This is the most interesting section of the trail, but it must be taken slowly and with care. The large rock formations with overhanging ledges look ideal for both bear dens and rattlesnakes, neither of which we saw when we visited in mid-April. But the intricate shapes of the rocks are almost canyonlike in some places. Small pockets of earth amid the boulders support tall rhododendrons and black cherry saplings. One boulder even has tiny rhododendrons sprouting out of it in a straight line about halfway down its face, where there appears to be no soil at all.

Finally, you emerge into a less rocky area. To the left a short path leads to an outcropping from which you can view the Connemaugh Gorge and River below. Then begins the steep descent back down to the valley. When you reach the stream, turn left a few hundred feet up to a log bridge. Cross the bridge and bear right back to the parking lot.

The Charles F. Lewis Natural Area, named for the first president of the Western Pennsylvania Conservancy, is a fitting monument to a dedicated conservationist. Although it seems wild and remote, it is less than eight miles from a city and easily accessible to those who want a quiet day in the outdoors.

From downtown Johnstown: Follow Route 403 north/56 west (Roosevelt Boulevard). After one mile the highway bears left at a fork. At 1.5 miles from downtown continue straight ahead on Route 403; .3 mile further follow 403 right across the bridge and then left again (Cooper Avenue). The Charles F. Lewis Natural Area is 7.2 miles from downtown Johnstown on the right side of Route 403. There is a prominent sign in the picnic area just before the wooden gateway into the woods.

40 MT. DAVIS NATURAL AREA

Mt. Davis Natural Area, in Somerset County near the Maryland border, marks the highest point in Pennsylvania. At 3,213 feet, it is the lowest high point in the Appalachian Mountain states. Located in the middle of the high, rolling Allegheny Plateau, Mt. Davis is part of 30-mile-long Negro Mountain, which lies between Laurel Mountain on the west and Allegheny Mountain on the east.

This 581-acre natural area in Forbes State Forest has a number of interesting trails, an unusual geologic formation, a heath barren, a rhododendron- and hemlock-lined stream, and several large rock outcroppings. Designated as a natural area in 1974, it is one of forty-four such ecologically significant areas in the state.

An easy, mostly level, three-mile-loop hike begins at the Mt. Davis picnic area, where you can park your car. Walk uphill (west) to High Point Trail and turn left. After an eighth of a mile, take the narrow Tub Mill Run Trail left for

Woodland pool, Mt. Davis Natural Area

a little over a quarter of a mile until it intersects with Shelter Rock Road. The road is closed to motorized vehicles and marks the eastern boundary of the natural area.

Turn right and follow the road for over a mile through a forest of red, scarlet, and white oaks, black birches, eastern hemlocks, cucumber, and sassafras trees. You will cross tributaries of Tub Mill Run twice before you reach Shelter Rock Trail on the right. The trail is rocky with a gentle slope and features a grove of pitch pines, dense rhododendron thickets, and a final crossing of Tub Mill Run. Several large boulders with ledges and crevices will be on your left as you make a short climb.

Once the trail levels off, the vegetation gets smaller. Because of repeated logging and burning, which destroyed the topsoil, what was once a forest has become a heath barren with stunted oak trees, pitch pines, black and yellow birch, quaking aspen, and black and fire cherry. The understory of mountain laurel, lowbush blueberry, scrub oak, greenbrier, teaberry, and several species of club moss is especially lovely in spring, when the trailing arbutus and painted trilliums are in bloom.

Turn right onto a paved road that leads to a forty-foot observation tower and a series of large, flat rocks with attached plaques that explain both the human history and natural features of the mountaintop. Mt. Davis is actually the single highest rock here and was named for the surveyor—John N. Davis—who determined it. Davis was also a naturalist and could identify all the plants and wildlife of the area. He was particularly interested in the "sorted stone patterns" on the ground.

The patterns are easier to see if you climb the observation tower and look north toward Negro Mountain. As a result of continual freezing and thawing during the late Pleistocene Age, less than 70,000 years ago, the Pottsville sandstone of the mountaintop was broken up to form stone circles. The patterns around Mt. Davis are probably the best examples of this geologic phenomenon in the Appalachian Mountains.

If visibility is good, the view of nearby ridges will be confusing. Many look higher than Mt. Davis, but that is merely an optical illusion since Negro Mountain, for a distance of five miles, is above three thousand feet.

You can follow the quarter-mile-long Mt. Davis Trail at the top if you have driven rather than walked to the high point. Otherwise, the mile-long High Point Trail back to the picnic area is a flat, easy walk through the heath barren.

We have visited Mt. Davis in summer and fall, and both times it was overcast and raining. In fact, the weather on top is often very cold, with frost during every month of the year and snow depths of three to four feet by midwinter. Late spring or early summer, when the wildflowers and shrubs are in bloom, would be the best times to visit.

From Johnstown: Follow U.S. 219 south 27 miles past Somerset. At the end of the freeway continue south on Route 219 for 17 miles to Meyersdale. Turn right. A sign says Mt. Davis High Point. Drive 3.3 miles and turn right. After 3.1 miles, bear right to a stop sign .9 mile further. Turn right again. At about 2.5 miles you will reach the Mt. Davis Picnic Area on your left.

41 FALLINGWATER

Fallingwater was architect Frank Lloyd Wright's "nature poem to modern man," according to his biographer, Robert C. Twombley. Located in southern Fayette County, it is seventy miles from Pittsburgh. Fallingwater was designed and built as a vacation home for Pittsburgh department-store owner Edgar J. Kaufmann and his wife in 1936, but since 1963 the house and grounds have been owned and operated by the Western Pennsylvania Conservancy.

For anyone interested in humanity's relationship to nature, a tour of Fallingwater and its grounds is an illuminating experience. However, you should make reservations by calling 412-329-8501 since space is limited. Tours of the house are conducted April through mid-November, Tuesday through Sunday,

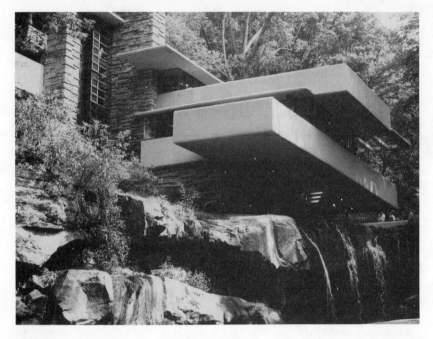

Fallingwater

from 10:00 A.M. until 4:00 P.M. Members of the Western Pennsylvania Conservancy receive two free admissions each year. Others, including children over ten, pay four dollars, with a fifty-cent discount during weekdays for senior citizens.

There are fewer visitors on weekdays, but free nature walks around the grounds are offered only on Saturday and Sunday afternoons at 1:15, 2:15, and 3:15 (May through October). A guide leads the easy, informative walk, pointing out the trees, wildflowers, and shrubs of the natural environment. The walk concludes at a southeast overlook of Fallingwater, a view that is not seen on the scheduled tour of the house.

No matter when you decide to visit, plan on arriving a half hour before the house tour so you will have time to study the excellent exhibit on Fallingwater that is part of the visitors pavilion. The pavilion also features an attractive gift shop, composting toilets in spotless restrooms, and a child-care center that charges one dollar per child per hour. (Children under ten years of age are not permitted on the tour.)

The hour-long house tour begins promptly and leads participants along paths through a woods of oak and beech, rhododendron and mountain laurel, the only "garden" Fallingwater has. Originally the Kaufmanns had envisioned a home with a view of the Bear Run waterfall, but Wright told them that "if you can see the waterfall, day after day, without any effort, it will soon grow boring."

Instead, he perched the house above the falls, building it of native stone and making it fit into the natural setting. He even refused to cut down trees where he planned to build walkways, and so the walks were constructed around the trees. As Edgar J. Kaufmann, Jr., explained when he presented Fallingwater to the Western Pennsylvania Conservancy as a memorial to his parents, "House and site together form the very image of man's desire to be at one with nature."

To get a good view of the house and waterfall, visitors must descend a steep path to the base of the falls and look up at them. In contrast, the entrance to the house, which is reached by crossing a bridge and approaching what looks like the back of Fallingwater, is not nearly as dramatic. But then Wright designed no grand staircases or imposing foyers for the house. The halls are narrow, dark, and cavelike, and the doorways into each room are abrupt divisions separating the dark halls from the light-flooded rooms. Windows sweep around corners, allowing "man to look out of the corner where he had never looked before," as Wright declared. Nothing is allowed to obstruct the view of the outdoors. The walls are constructed of horizontally laid rocks reinforced with concrete that is ochre-colored to blend into the earth.

The large living room, the focal point of the house, is built around a rocky ledge, now serving as the hearthstone of a huge fireplace. The rest of the floor is flagstone that is regularly polished with wax to make the stones look wet, just as they do in a rocky mountain stream. Wright wanted to make it difficult to decide where the outside stopped and the inside began. The furnishings, too, blend with the environment, and many were especially designed by Wright for Fallingwater. But the Kaufmanns' tastes are also evident. Window frames are painted Cherokee red, Mr. Kaufmann's favorite color, and a snake motif reflects Mrs. Kaufmann's interests.

The tour guides explain special features in each room, answer questions, and are able to discuss everything from the Picasso prints on the walls to the Lipchitz sculptures on the grounds. In fact, the house tour is as much a short introduction to art and architecture as it is a lesson on the harmonious relationship possible between man and nature.

Lunch is available at a small cafe in the pavilion, but if you want to picnic there are facilities at nearby Ohiopyle State Park. If you eat at Fallingwater, however, you can then take the natural-history walk before exploring some of the twenty miles of trails at nearby Bear Run Nature Reserve, also owned by the Conservancy.

Exit from Fallingwater back onto Pa. Route 381 and turn left. At .5 mile take a right into the parking lot behind the farmhouse labeled Bear Run Nature Reserve. Here you can pick up easy-to-follow trail maps.

Our family particularly enjoyed the three-mile-long Peninsula Trail across the highway. It leads over a wide meadow and then bears left around a peninsula that juts out above the Youghiogheny River. The trail is steep and rocky in places, but with good hiking shoes the average walker should have no trouble. Several overlooks give spectacular views of the river. After two miles, you will pass an obvious campsite on your left between the trail and the river. Several hundred feet beyond that, turn right on Saddle Trail. This trail ascends a fairly steep hill and rejoins a short section of Peninsula Trail, which you followed earlier near the beginning of the walk. Instead of taking it back to the highway, turn left on Kinglet Trail and finish your hike by enjoying the pine plantation the trail intersects.

The best times to visit Fallingwater and Bear Run Nature Reserve are in May or June, when the wildflowers are in bloom and it is still cool enough to enjoy hiking, or in October, in time for the autumn color. Fallingwater is not air-conditioned, and on the hundred-degree, humid day in August when we visited, it was quite uncomfortable.

Fallingwater welcomes group reservations, making it an excellent place to take school classes, garden clubs, and nature-oriented organizations as well as families. Bear Run Nature Reserve has a wide variety of short, easy trails for all ages.

Fallingwater is a Pennsylvania treasure both for its architectural renown and for its natural beauty. Edgar J. Kaufmann, Jr., described it well when he said that Fallingwater's "beauty remains fresh like that of the nature into which it fits."

From Pittsburgh: Take Route 51 south to Uniontown. Then follow Route 40 east to Farmington. Take Route 381 north to Ohiopyle. Three miles north of Ohiopyle turn left off 381 into Fallingwater.

42 OHIOPYLE STATE PARK

Ohiopyle State Park, directly south of Fallingwater in Fayette and Somerset counties, has something for almost everyone. White-water boating enthusiasts know it as the place to run the Youghiogheny Gorge. Naturalists go there to walk the trails in the Ferncliff Natural Area. People who appreciate scenic beauty are drawn to the Ohiopyle Falls, as well as to a view of nearby Cucumber Falls on Cucumber Run just before it joins the "Yough." And last, but not least, hikers, bikers, and cross-country skiers are enthusiastic about the

Great falls of the Youghiogheny (Ohiopyle Falls), Ohiopyle State Park

newly opened, nine-mile-long trail on the abandoned Western Maryland Railway right-of-way, which takes them up the gorge from the village of Ohiopyle.

The 18,463-acre park and the two adjacent state game lands are known as the gateway to the Laurel Mountains—a place of wild scenic beauty primarily because of the 1,700-foot-deep Youghiogheny Gorge, formed by the river cutting through Laurel Ridge. The best place to see the geologic forces that cut the gorge still at work is at the Ohiopyle Falls Day Use Area off Pa. 381, directly across the road from the village of Ohiopyle. There you will find platforms that overlook the rushing water and realize why the Indians named the area Ohiopehhle, which means "white frothy water." In this area the river flows over a resistant sandstone but has cut through the surrounding, softer shale, so that the water now tumbles over wide sandstone ledges.

In the nineteenth century, the famous English geologist Charles Lyell visited and sketched the falls. By the early twentieth century, it was a summer resort area serviced by special excursion trains on the Baltimore and Ohio Railroad out of Pittsburgh. Five hotels catered to a summer tourist population of between ten and twelve thousand, but the wealthy were partial to Fern Cliff

Park, now part of the Ferncliff Natural Area, and the next place to visit on your tour of the park.

Turn and drive back across the river on Pa. 381 and pull off left into the parking area, where the trail begins. The natural area is actually a two-hundred-acre peninsula made of the same resistant Pottsville sandstone that you saw at the falls. For this reason, the river, as it loops around the peninsula, drops ninety feet in less than two miles, first at the falls (which you can see from Ferncliff) and then along the extremely turbulent rapids.

The Ferncliff peninsula is known as the meeting place of northern and southern plants, including the interesting shrub buffalo nut, a root parasite on other shrubs and trees with small, pale green flowers that bloom in short clusters in May. Its pear-shaped, leathery, inch-long, yellowish-green fruit, containing one large, poisonous, oily seed, gives the shrub its alternate name—oilnut.

Two of the southern wildflowers that reach their northernmost limit on Ferncliff are Barbara's buttons, or large-flowered marshallia, and Carolina tassel-rue, or false bugbane. Barbara's buttons, which blooms at the end of June and the beginning of July, has a pink flower the size and shape of a dandelion, lancelike, three-ribbed leaves, and a one-to-three-foot stem. Carolina tassel-rue blossoms in midsummer with round, white, composite flowers on a separate flower stem. In addition, the usual ephemeral wildflowers, such as white clintonia, trailing arbutus, and false Solomon's seal, can be found here in the spring.

Although Ferncliff is primarily a northern oak forest, the more southerly umbrella magnolias thrive in the understory. And, of course, Ferncliff has several fern species, with Christmas, marginal wood, and spinulose woodferns growing thickly on the forest floor, and royal and cinnamon ferns along the river.

Ferncliff Trail circles the peninsula and provides several good views along the way, including the Lewis Hines Memorial Overlook. It is wise to stay on the trail since the understory is often thick with ferns and/or poison ivy. At least one copperhead snake also lives here because one struck at me in the middle of the path on a late spring day. Luckily, it missed, posed for photos, and then slithered off down the steep bank toward the river. Other wildlife I observed were innumerable eastern chipmunks, blue-gray gnatcatchers, eastern pewees, and cedar waxwings.

From Ferncliff return to the falls area on Pa. 381 and continue on the highway south for less than a mile until you reach a fork in the road. Turn right onto Legislative Route 26071 and drive another half mile until you see a parking area on the left. Pull in, park, cross the road, and take the steps leading down to Cucumber Falls.

The Western Pennsylvania Conservancy, whose efforts in the late 1940s, 1950s, and 1960s finally resulted in the purchase of all the pieces of land needed to complete the park's boundaries, considers the Cucumber Falls area to be as botanically interesting as Ferncliff but for different reasons. Unlike Ferncliff, which has a dry woods, the Cucumber Falls Ravine—and indeed much of the rest of the park—is moister, making it attractive to white basswood, a tree common to the southern Appalachians. Blue monkshood, which blooms from mid-August through early September, is abundant at the mouth of Cucumber Run, and with its five irregular, petal-like, deep blue sepals, the upper of which is shaped like a helmet or hood, it is a striking wildflower. American bugbane, closely related to black cohosh or bugbane, is also common around Cucumber Falls. The falls itself is thirty feet high, ten feet higher than Ohiopyle Falls, and nestled in a ravine thick with rhododendron bushes.

Finally, to reach the new Youghiogheny River Trail, drive back to Ohiopyle. Just before crossing the river on Pa. 381, turn right at Ohiopyle's old railroad station, now being restored to provide comfort facilities and information to park visitors. You can park here as well as at the end of the trail, nine miles southeast near Confluence. The trail itself is wide and level and gives the hiker outstanding views of the river, feeder streams, and surrounding forest.

Many days can be spent exploring the park because there are numerous scenic overlooks, waterfalls, forty miles of day trails, camping and picnicking facilities, a nature center, and interpretive programs, in addition to the park's largest attraction—white-water boating. Four park concessionaires cater to people interested in boating, but since the demand is high it is wise to make reservations. A daily river quota allows 960 persons by the concessionaires and 960 private, unguided boaters. For information write the Ohiopyle State Park, P.O. Box 105, Ohiopyle, PA 15470, or call 412-329-4707 and ask for the "Boating/Camping Reservations" brochure.

The best time to visit the park is late spring and summer, when the weather is warm enough to enjoy boating and the southern wildflowers are at their height. But since it is crowded then, if you are content to walk, late fall and early spring might provide a quieter experience. For groups a park naturalist is available to lead nature walks and present environmentally oriented programs if you make arrangements ahead of time. A tour of Ferncliff is especially nice—our Altoona-based Audubon Society has twice combined a day trip to Fallingwater with a naturalist-led walk over Ferncliff.

Ohiopyle State Park was finally dedicated in May 31, 1971, and today it attracts over a million and a half visitors a year. Yet the area is so large that you can easily find solitude.

From Pittsburgh: Follow the directions in Chapter 41 on Fallingwater; three miles before the entrance to Fallingwater, you will reach the village of Ohiopyle.

43 TRILLIUM TRAIL

Spring in an eastern forest is a special season for people who like wildflowers. Before the leaves emerge on the trees and shade the forest floor, a wide variety of spring ephemerals bloom. The five species of trilliums that grow in Pennsylvania's woods are always favorites, and to find even a scattering of the showy plants is a treat.

But along Trillium Trail in Allegheny County northeast of Pittsburgh, the trillium-lover is overwhelmed by the sight of tens of thousands of white trilliums (*Trillium grandiflorum*) covering a hillside above a narrow ravine. When the trilliums bloom in early May, families with children, old couples and young, and individual wildflower-fanciers all stroll along the half-mile trail, bending down to read every small label in front of many wildflower species, including a predominantly yellowish-white variety of purple trillium (*Trillium erectum*) that sharp-eyed people notice is mixed in with the white trilliums.

The only real noise comes from traffic on the winding road that parallels the trail. A parking lot at either end of the trail makes it possible to put a car at either end, so you don't have to retrace your steps; but the trail is so short, easy, and lovely that, unless you have very little strength, it is worth it to walk over it twice.

Trillium grandiflorum, a member of the lily family, is also called white wood lily. It has one large, showy white flower that grows on a stalk up to three inches long. Trillium comes from the word "trifolium," meaning three-leaved, and, in fact, its leaves, sepals, and petals come in threes, an easy way to identify the plant. In addition, the white flower of *Trillium grandiflorum* turns pink as it ages.

To see the trillium display, start at the north parking lot. As you walk on the wide path that leads to the trail, notice the Virginia bluebells (*Mertensia virginica*) growing there. Turn left onto Trillium Trail and watch carefully for such wildflowers as cut-leaved toothwort, spring beauties, large-flowered bellwort, wild ginger, false Solomon's seal, trout lilies, skunk cabbage, white clintonia, hepatica, bishop's cap, jack-in-the-pulpit, and Virginia waterleaf growing amid the sea of white and green *Trillium grandiflorum*. Occasional small streams trickle off the hillside to join the stream that runs between road and trail.

There is no way you can get lost on the well-labeled trail. When you reach its southern terminus, you can sit on the wooden benches at the top of the steps that lead down to and then over the stream to the second parking lot. It is possible to walk back along the road, but since traffic is swift taking the trail is a better choice.

Trillium grandiflorum, Trillium Trail

The first two weeks in May, depending on the weather, are the only time to visit Trillium Trail. Of course, it is a lovely ravine and a pleasant walk anytime if you happen to live locally, but if you are coming from a distance it makes sense to plan a trip to Pittsburgh during this period.

Trillium Trail is a wonderful place to take garden clubs. The trail is so short and easy that the members can dress well enough to go to one of Pittsburgh's fine restaurants afterward. There are no picnic areas or public facilities of any kind at the trail.

From Pittsburgh: Follow the Allegheny Valley Expressway (Pa. 28). Exit onto Fox Chapel Road. Follow it north .9 mile. Turn left onto Squaw Run Road. Proceed 1 mile. Take left fork .2 mile to parking lot for Trillium Trail or continue a half mile further up the road for the north part of the trail.

44 BEECHWOOD FARMS NATURE RESERVE

Beechwood Farms Nature Reserve, only eight miles northeast of Pittsburgh, is the largest private nature reserve in western Pennsylvania. Owned by the Western Pennsylvania Conservancy and maintained and operated by the Audubon Society of Western Pennsylvania, it features more than five miles of trails through a varied terrain.

The trails are open from dawn until dusk year-round, but the Evans Nature Center, which contains an excellent book and gift shop, a wildlife observation room, a two-hundred-seat auditorium, an open-barn meeting area, and nature displays, is open Tuesday through Saturday from 9:00 A.M. until 5:00 P.M. and Sunday from 1:00 P.M. to 5:00 P.M. There you can pick up a map and learn from the gregarious volunteers who operate the Owl's Nest gift shop what programs and special events are available. Since their goal is "to make the public aware of the importance of ecologically sound stewardship of the land and to foster understanding and appreciation of the environment," they offer a variety of year-round programs for people of all ages and for all segments of the community, including preschoolers, school and youth groups, families, and teachers.

Originally the nature center was part of the Flynn estate, built as a family home in 1870. Later it served as a boardinghouse for laborers on what had become a very large farm. Today outside the center are an herb garden and a "natural lawn" area. Nearby you can observe an operating wind generator and study the explanatory display. Then pick up Goldenrod Trail, which begins behind the nature center and leads to a pond whose chief attraction is a small flock of very cooperative and photogenic Canada geese.

Goldenrod Trail leads into Violet Trail, which in turn joins Spring Hollow Trail. Along this latter, deeply wooded trail in spring, a large variety of wildflowers, such as rue anemone, jack-in-the-pulpit, Solomon's seal, purple trillium, wood anemone, skunk cabbage, and large white-flowered trillium, grow beneath the black and white oaks. A hillside of purple violets and numerous dogwood trees add to the ambience of the scene. Rufous-sided towhees, blue-gray gnatcatchers, American redstarts, yellow warblers, northern cardinals, ovenbirds, and yellow-shafted flickers are just a few of the birds you may see or hear in the woods. One pair of red-tailed hawks nests in an old white oak near the trail, and both the parents and the nest can be observed from Spring Hollow Trail in late winter and early spring.

Eventually Spring Hollow Trail merges into Meadow View Trail, which is more open and is marked, at the beginning, with a grove of spiny-trunked Hercules'-club trees. Covered with lush white flowers in the summer and deep

Evans Nature Center, Beechwood Farms Nature Reserve

purple berries, relished by robins and cedar waxwings, in the fall, these rather peculiar-looking, eight-to-ten-foot-high trees also boast enormous composite leaves that experts claim are the largest of any tree in North America. In addition, an old apple orchard in an overgrown meadow is a cloud of pink and white in spring and filled with food for white-tailed deer in the fall. Field sparrows and white-throated sparrows also enjoy the area.

Turn right onto Pine Hollow Trail. Once again the surroundings change, this time back to a wooded environment. The attraction in the middle of this trail is Beechwood Falls. Beyond that, climb up through a planting of red pines that is thirty-five to forty years old judging from the height of the trees.

Eventually the trail joins the other end of Meadow View Trail. After a couple hundred feet a short offshoot leads to Meadow View Lookout, which provides a nice overlook of the gently rolling countryside. Wood thrushes sing their ethereal songs off in the distance on beautiful May and June days.

In 1984 the Conservancy purchased an additional piece of property, bringing the reserve's total acreage to 120. Part of the land is an upland plateau of abandoned fields reverting to woodland, where blue-winged and golden-winged warblers can be seen. Another section is a maturing spruce plantation interspersed with deciduous trees.

But the focal point of the acquisition is a mature stand of mixed-oak forest, containing some trees that are several hundred years old. In this area, hooded warblers and American redstarts are the birds to look for, and plume lily, small-flowered crowfoot, wild geranium, and spinulose woodfern are some of the wild plants that grow beneath the oak trees. Several more loop trails are scheduled to be built through this new plot.

Despite being surrounded by suburban Fox Chapel, Beechwood Farms gives little indication of the more urbanized world beyond its perimeter. Certainly such a natural oasis so near a major city can provide a wonderful change of pace for urban dwellers and should inspire them to become Friends of Beechwood. Not only does a membership help maintain Beechwood Farms Nature Reserve, but members receive the informative, seasonal *Beechwood Barker,* a newsletter that highlights nature studies as well as the events scheduled throughout the year. Members also may use the reserve's fine natural-history library, which is well stocked with classic nature books and reference sources.

Even if you are not a member, you can enjoy the Beechwood Farms Nature Reserve in every season of the year. If you call 412-963-6100 or write Beechwood Farms, 614 Dorseyville Road, Pittsburgh, PA 15238, well in advance, the two naturalists there will be happy to lead your group around the reserve.

From Pittsburgh: Follow the Allegheny Valley Expressway (Pa. 28). Exit onto Fox Chapel Road north. After .9 mile turn left onto Squaw Run Road. After 1.1 miles take another left fork. Proceed uphill 1.1 miles to Dorseyville Road. Turn right onto Dorseyville Road (north). Proceed 1.8 miles. Beechwood Farms is on the left.

45 ENLOW FORK NATURAL AREA

Enlow Fork Natural Area, along the border of Washington and Greene counties in southwestern Pennsylvania, was purchased by the Western Pennsylvania Conservancy in 1986 and resold to the Pennsylvania Game Commission as State Game Lands 302. The Game Commission agreed to protect the unusual diversity of wildflowers, ferns, shrubs, and trees, in addition to man-

Sycamore trees along Enlow Fork, Enlow Fork Natural Area

aging the abundant wildlife, which includes mink, beaver, white-tailed deer, raccoons, and game- and songbirds.

Because of Enlow Fork's location near the West Virginia border, its flora includes both southern and midwestern species. Trees such as yellow oak, yellow buckeye, redbud, and pawpaw are abundant on the wooded hillsides, as are the more common (to Pennsylvania) white, chestnut, and red oaks. Magnificent old sycamore trees, some more than five feet in diameter, line the banks of Enlow Fork, a sparkling, broad trout stream stocked each spring by the Pennsylvania Fish Commission. The stream is also clean enough to support rock bass and a good population of naturally reproducing smallmouth bass.

Wildflowers, many of which are rare to the state, cover the banks along the sanctuary's single gravel road as well as the streambanks. Blue-eyed Mary, a plant of the central United States, carpets the ground in May. Both blue-eyed Mary and Riddell's hedge nettle—a species mainly found in the southern Appalachians that blooms in June and July and is also found at Enlow Fork— were recently added to the Pennsylvania Plants of Special Concern list.

As you follow the stream in search of wildflowers in April and May, you will discover other treasures, such as both red and white trillium, wild ginger, pale violets, star-of-Bethlehem, dame's rocket, and a pale pink valerian (*Valeriana pauciflora*). In July and August great blue lobelia and wild bergamot bloom. The wooded banks along the road are colorful in mid-May with the pale blue blossoms of appendaged waterleaf and blue phlox, the white bells of Solomon's seal, and the white sprays of false Solomon's seal, along with the red-and-gold columbines, the bright red fire pinks, and the yellow of lesser celandine and golden ragwort. Earlier in the season, twinleaf and spring (or dwarf) larkspur are among the more striking flowers.

Fern fanciers will delight in Enlow because the exposed rock ledges, large limestone outcroppings, and talus slopes throughout the steep valley are excellent places to see two uncommon fern species—walking and bulblet ferns.

Then there are the birds and butterflies. In May the valley reverberates with bird song from dawn until dusk, without the customary midday respite songbirds usually take. During our visit the predominant singers were northern orioles, yellow warblers, and blue-gray gnatcatchers, but we also identified twenty-eight other species, including a yellow-breasted chat, black-billed cuckoo, scarlet tanager, red-eyed vireo, ruby-throated hummingbird, Carolina chickadee, and both the Acadian and least flycatchers. However, we did not find the yellow-throated warbler, which, along with the Carolina chickadee, is a southern bird species that comes to breed as far north as Enlow.

Probably because the valley has been so isolated, it has escaped the pesticidal sprayings that are so common now to keep suburban lawns and country farms weed-free and that have diminished the state's butterfly population. That was why the sight of dozens of tiger and spicebush swallowtails on every exposed mud flat along the creek, plus a wide variety of other butterfly species feeding on the abundant valerian and dame's rocket, was a highlight of our visit to Enlow Fork.

Since there are no facilities at Enlow, it is advisable to pack a box lunch and carry along a canteen. Trails, too, are nonexistent, but if you follow the streambank in as far as you want to go (it is more than 3.5 miles from where you park your car to the end of the thousand-acre property) and then walk back along the gravel road, there is no chance of getting lost. On a hot day wear an old pair of sneakers and shorts and wade up the streambed. You will see tadpoles, frogs, and schools of fry and stay cool besides.

From Pittsburgh: Take Interstate 279 south across the Fort Pitt Bridge. After 5.8 miles connect with Interstate 79 south toward Washington, Pa. Drive 20.3 miles south, connect with Interstate 70 west, and proceed 11.6 miles to the Claysville exit (Exit 2). At the stop sign at the bottom of the exit ramp, turn right and right again on U.S. 40 east toward Claysville. At the center of town, .8 mile, turn right just beyond Sacred Heart Church on Pa. 231 south. At 3.5 miles from Claysville take the farthest right turn toward Good Intent and West Finley. Ignore the right turn into Good Intent, 4.2 miles from Pa. 231, and continue straight ahead into West Finley another 3.7 miles. At the stop sign in West Finley bear left toward Graysville. Cross the bridge over Enlow Fork after 2.4 miles and turn right immediately onto a small steel bridge. Follow the dirt road 1.6 miles; then make a very sharp right onto another dirt road, which leads downhill 1.3 miles to a pull-off beside the remnants of a washed-out bridge. Park here and begin your walk downstream.

46 RACCOON CREEK STATE PARK

Raccoon Creek State Park, only twenty-five miles west of Pittsburgh, has many attractions for the nature enthusiast. The Wildflower Reserve on its eastern end and Frankfort Mineral Springs at its western border provide interesting walks through wooded stream environments where wildflowers and birds are abundant.

The center of the park is dominated by Raccoon Lake, popular with fishermen and birdwatchers. At the western arm of the lake two short, unnamed trails begin, as well as the mile-and-a-half Valley Trail. But the best walking is at the Wildflower Reserve and the Frankfort Mineral Springs, both of which were originally purchased by the Western Pennsylvania Conservancy and later turned over to the park.

As you enter the park from the east on U.S. 30, watch to the right for a hidden entrance labeled Wildflower Reserve. Park in the lot and stop first at the nature center to pick up wildflower brochures and a park map. During the

Trout lily, Raccoon Creek State Park

spring and summer park naturalists lead walks through the reserve; these can be helpful as well as fun since many eyes are better than two in spotting birds and some of the more retiring wildflowers, such as wild ginger. Then, too, the guides will be able to point out, for instance, the difference between Dutchman's-breeches and squirrel corn and to relate some of the folklore connected with many of our native wildflowers.

Called by one naturalist "Nature's most beautiful wildflower garden in Western Pennsylvania," the Wildflower Reserve has a unique habitat that allows many characteristically southern and midwestern species, like snow trillium, harbinger-of-spring, and miami-mist, to extend their range into southwestern Pennsylvania.

If you decide to explore the area on your own, begin on Jennings Trail near the nature center and continue behind the old Hungerford Cabin, a 150-year-old cabin-farmhouse. Jennings Trail, named for Dr. O. E. Jennings, a western Pennsylvania botanist, parallels Route 30 until the trail drops down on wooden steps to the creek bottomland. Then it follows the stream for a little more than half a mile until it joins Old Wagon Trail, a shorter trail that also begins near the nature center and similarly drops down to the creek. It is possible to take Old Wagon Trail back up to the nature center if you want to walk only a mile. But you see a greater variety of wildflowers if you continue along the flat creek bed on Jennings Trail for another mile.

Raccoon Creek is on the right, while steep, rocky ledges loom above you on the left. In spring five species of trilliums—the snow, purple, great white, sessile, and nodding (or drooping) trillium—cover the ledge side with thousands of blooms. Along the creek, beds of yellow trout lilies contrive to blossom just as trout season begins in Pennsylvania.

At the junction of Jennings Trail with Audubon Trail, turn left up Audubon Trail to a high hogback ridge that runs for half a mile back to the nature center. From here you can look down on treetops and get excellent views of birds from above. In early May this area is filled with yellow warblers and scarlet tanagers.

Many hours can be spent wandering the trails of the Wildflower Reserve. Then, if you plan to stay only a day at the park, drive to the lake for a picnic since the nearest restaurant is seven miles to the east.

After lunch continue to the western end of the park until you reach Pa. 18. Turn left and drive less than a half mile to a parking lot on the right. From here you can follow a short, scenic trail around the Frankfort Mineral Springs area, the site of a nationally known health spa during the 1800s. The trail meanders beside a beautiful woodland stream that culminates in a semicircular rock ledge with a lovely waterfall. Then take the trail that leads right, up out of the streambed, to a historic museum, which is open during the summer. It is possible to retrace your steps to your car after visiting the museum. A longer alternative is to walk behind the museum and follow the section of Mineral Springs Trail that parallels Pa. 18 and ends at the park office. Then walk back along the edge of the highway to your car, a mile-long circuit. In May there are almost as many wildflowers in this area as are found in the Wildflower Reserve, and the added attraction of a waterfall makes this a nice ending to the day.

Both family and group camping facilities are available at Raccoon Creek State Park, and boating is allowed on the lake. Arrangements to have a park naturalist lead a group tour can be made by calling the Wildflower Reserve at 412-899-3611 or the Park Office at 412-899-2200 several weeks ahead of the busy spring season. (Weekdays are less busy and easier to schedule.)

From April to September the reserve has dozens of flowering species. In the first week of May more than thirty species of wildflowers bloom, including cut-leaved hepatica, spring beauty, bloodroot, woodland phlox, blue cohosh, wood and rue anemones, and several species of violets. But in the summer four species of orchids—pale green orchis, nodding ladies tresses, downy rattlesnake plantain, and the large twayblade—can be found, in addition to other showy flowers, like the cardinal flower and the great lobelia. The parasitic plants Indian pipe and pinesap are also summer flowers, while the lovely closed gentian ends the blooming season in September.

Summer is the best time to make use of the guided tours and the historic museum at Frankfort Mineral Springs. If you are a fern enthusiast, the Wildflower Reserve boasts twenty-eight species, including the unique walking fern; the narrow-leaved, silvery, maidenhair, and ebony spleenworts; and the cut-leaved, coarse-lobed, and matricary grape ferns. All are at their best in summer. Of course, if you live in the Pittsburgh area, monthly excursions from April through September are the best way to see the medley of flowers that makes Raccoon Creek State Park famous.

From downtown Pittsburgh: Cross the Fort Pitt Bridge. Continue through the Fort Pitt Tunnel on Interstate 279 south and U.S. 22–30 west. At 5.4 miles from the bridge, the highway intersects Interstate 79. Continue west on U.S. 22–30 toward the Pittsburgh International Airport. Drive 4.3 miles further west before exiting off the highway to the right to continue west on U.S. 22–30. (Do not continue straight ahead toward the airport.) Continue westbound for 3.9 miles. Exit off the highway to follow U.S. 30 west through the town of Imperial. At 9.5 miles from the exit off Route 22, watch for hidden entrance to the right just over the hill for the Wildflower Reserve.

47 TODD SANCTUARY

The Todd Sanctuary in southeastern Butler County is owned and operated by the Audubon Society of Western Pennsylvania. Named for W. E. Clyde Todd, the former bird curator at the Carnegie Museum who donated the first parcel of land in 1942, Todd Sanctuary has 160 acres of wooded ravines,

Watson's Run, Todd Sanctuary

fields, and streams crisscrossed by five miles of well-maintained trails that are open free to the public from dawn until dusk.

Turn left past the bulletin board at the parking lot and follow the trail right above the stream until it reaches a wooden bridge labeled McCrey's Crossing. Cross the bridge to the old cabin, the focal point of the sanctuary, where the major trails begin. In the yard are two picnic tables, drinking water, and latrines—the only facilities available on the property.

Walk left behind the cabin and take the yellow-blazed Loop Trail, which leads past some magnificent old hemlocks and white oaks with a thick under-story of ferns. Near the site of an old quarry on the left is a large stand of cut-leaved grape ferns on both sides of the trail. These triangular-leaved ferns are extremely variable in shape, so look for the lacy-cut, sterile leaves as well as the coarser leaf that grows on the same stalk as the distinctive spore case. In spring the woods also support jack-in-the-pulpit and several species of violets, and in late summer you can find white snakeroot and the miniscule yellow flowers of agrimony.

After passing Warbler and Indian Pipe trails on the right, you will reach Meadow Trail. You can either turn right and then left on Meadow Trail or continue on Loop Trail. Either way will bring you to a pond tucked in an old meadow with several species of goldenrod, joe-pye weed, New York ironweed, steeplebush, and field milkwort in early September.

This area is also attractive to birds. Ruby-throated hummingbirds, cedar waxwings, gray catbirds, and northern cardinals are just a few of the 214 species that have been identified in the Todd Sanctuary during the seventy years since W. E. Clyde Todd began keeping a bird list. The mud at the edge of the pond is a mosaic of deer tracks, and along the trails is evidence of deer having grazed on the vegetation.

After circling the pond, proceed along Loop Trail through a very large hawthorn thicket and then past a magnificent Scotch pine. Soon you will again be in deep woods, where eastern chipmunks, eastern pewees, black-capped chickadees, and white-breasted nuthatches are abundant. The woods contain a variety of wildflowers, from the spring-blossoming white clintonia, mayapples, Solomon's seal, and trailing arbutus through summer's Indian pipes, white wood asters, and white baneberries.

Although you may not have been aware of it, the trail has been climbing steadily. It reaches a climax at what is called Inspiration Point, where you can look straight down to Watson's Run a couple hundred feet below. From Inspiration Point follow Loop Trail until it intersects with Ravine Trail. Turn left on Ravine Trail, which follows and often crosses the stream, and continue on the trail until it intersects with the well-marked sanctuary boundary line. Then you must retrace your steps, but it is worth it since this trail is the nicest on the property. Large rock outcroppings rear up along Watson's Run, and beside the stream a lovely selection of spring wildflowers grows—skunk cab-bage, hepatica, bloodroot, trillium, foamflower, and false Solomon's seal. Rat-tlesnake fern, as well as the more common Christmas, sensitive, and wood-ferns, also thrives here. Wood thrushes and ruffed grouse by the dozen were the predominant birds when we visited.

Following the signs take Ravine Trail all the way back to the cabin past the old mill site where Hesselgesser and Watson runs meet. By then you will have walked almost three easy miles. But a further half mile will take you right back along the portion of Loop Trail that you missed and then left on a portion of Polypody Trail. This trail is interesting because it passes several boulders that support large colonies of the dainty, evergreen polypody ferns. Turn left onto Indian Pipe Trail and follow it back to Loop Trail, where you started.

The Todd Sanctuary is only an hour's drive from Pittsburgh. If you're planning a visit, write to the Audubon Society of Western Pennsylvania (Beechwood Farms Nature Reserve, 614 Dorseyville Road, Pittsburgh, PA 15238) and ask for a trail map of the Todd Sanctuary. (There were none at the cabin when we visited. In fact, although it was Labor Day weekend, we saw only five other people during our five hours of exploration.)

This is an excellent place to take children because the trails are so easy. If you want to walk Ravine Trail, stream crossings are easiest in late summer and early fall.

From Pittsburgh: Take the Allegheny Valley Expressway (Route 28) north for 25 miles. Turn left onto Route 356 and drive .9 mile until you reach a cinema on your left. Turn right onto Monroe Road and proceed 1.3 miles over railroad tracks. Monroe branches off just before a golf course on the right. Take Kepple Road a further 1.9 miles until you reach the entrance to Todd Sanctuary on the right.

48 McCONNELLS MILL STATE PARK

McConnells Mill State Park, located in Lawrence County forty miles north of Pittsburgh, includes 2,512 acres of spectacular Slippery Rock Gorge. This gorge was formed twenty thousand years ago when the Wisconsin ice sheet, which had advanced to within a mile of the present mill, began melting. Previously the ice had dammed up Muddy Creek and Slippery Rock Creek, creating two large glacial lakes, Lake Edmund and Lake Arthur. Once the ice started melting, Lake Arthur began draining into the channel of Slippery Rock Creek, sending a large amount of water over the edge of the Homewood sandstone formation at what is today called Alpha Pass in the park. Within a hundred years the gorge had been deepened to four hundred feet by the rushing waters, and house-sized sandstone boulders had slid down into the gorge.

Today at McConnells Mill State Park you can see geologic features like crossbeds, which are minor layers of sediment lying at an angle to the usual horizontal layers in the sandstone rock. They were formed when currents

The old mill, McConnells Mill State Park

moved the loose sand and gravel of a streambed into ripples in the Slippery Rock area 300 million years ago. You can also immerse yourself in the more recent history of a beautifully preserved gristmill built in 1868 to make use of the rushing stream waters.

After turning left off U.S. 422 into the park, drive along the park road for six-tenths of a mile until you reach a parking place on the right for Alpha Pass (the name of a waterfall). From the fenced-off top you can look down at the thin stream of water disappearing into the treetops, or, if you are somewhat agile, you can walk to the left side of the parking lot and take a trail down past wooden railings, which, if gripped tightly, can help you over this short but steep part of the path. In less than one-tenth of a mile, turn right on a level trail that winds past huge, lichen-covered boulders to a breathtaking view of the falls, its plunge pool, and the surrounding truck-sized rocks.

Return to your car and proceed another half mile to an area designated for mill parking. Behind the restrooms is a steep but well-made path down to the mill. There is a road to the mill, but it and parking places at the mill are reserved for the elderly and the handicapped.

Free guided tours of the restored mill are conducted several times each day from Memorial Day through Labor Day, but it is also possible to wander through the mill on your own to view the machinery and read the labels. In addition to the mill, history buffs can enjoy walking over the beautiful and unusual Howe-Truss-type covered bridge, built in 1874 and still in use today, just below the mill area.

After leaving the mill, take a right turn (downstream) and enter the woods at a sign marking the Kildoo Nature Trail. A short section is paved so that even a person in a wheelchair can enjoy it, and during summer weekends the park naturalist leads several daily nature walks. You can explore the trail on your own since a free brochure available at the mill explains the paved part of the Kildoo Trail and provides a map of the entire two-mile circuit.

Plan on spending two to three hours if you decide to walk the whole trail, because once you leave the paved area the path is rocky, although easily negotiated if you take your time. Also, the beautiful views of Slippery Rock Creek and its tumble of boulders may tempt you to detour down to the creek for a closer look. Then, too, you will find yourself stopping to admire the wide variety of ferns and wildflowers along the trail.

Hemlock trees line the ravine, and American yew, an evergreen shrub, grows on top of the rocks. These rocks, in fact, support a myriad of interesting plant life—the wildflower wood sorrel, a variety of lichens, and the most common of the ferns that can be found along the trail, the common polypody. The more than twenty species of ferns that flourish along the Kildoo Trail include the bulblet, maidenhair, ebony spleenwort, marginal woodfern, fragile fern, and cut-leaved grape fern.

The wildflowers are also abundant, and in spring white clintonia, wild ginger, foamflower, sharp-lobed hepatica, false mitrewort, Solomon's seal, and Canada mayflower, among others, grow beside the trail. Summer finds some sections ablaze with cardinal flowers and wild bergamot. The pastel shades of nodding wild onions form several attractive beds, and the ghostly white of Indian pipes contrasts with the lush green of the forest floor.

Spring and summer are the best seasons to visit McConnells Mill State Park if you want to see the dazzling array of ferns and wildflowers or take guided tours through the mill. There is no swimming or camping, but there is picnicking at two designated areas. Other sports permitted in season and with proper gear are rock climbing, fishing, hunting, and white-water boating.

One of our recent visits was on a blazing midsummer day, when we found a walk along the Kildoo Nature Trail an excellent way to stay reasonably cool. The combination of geologic features, hiking trails, plants, and human history makes the park attractive to a wide spectrum of groups. You can also get off-season tours of the mill for your group if you call 412-368-8091 and make an appointment.

From Pittsburgh: Follow Interstate 79 for 40 miles north. Exit onto U.S. 422. Continue 1.8 miles west on 422. Turn left at sign for McConnells Mill State Park.

49 JENNINGS ENVIRONMENTAL EDUCATION CENTER

Jennings Environmental Education Center, located twelve miles north of Butler in western Pennsylvania, features a relict prairie, the eastern massasauga rattlesnake, and a spectacular prairie wildflower—the blazing star. It also has more than ten miles of trails and an excellent series of nature-oriented programs that are free to the public. Owned and operated by the Pennsylvania Bureau of State Parks, Jennings has three aims: "to protect natural ecosystems, manage park resources, and educate the public about various aspects of our environment through interpretation and environmental education programming."

The relict-prairie ecosystem of Jennings was discovered in 1902 by botanist Otto Emery Jennings of Pittsburgh's Carnegie Museum. But how had a prairie come to exist in wooded Pennsylvania? Geologists learned that during the last two glacial periods ice had covered the Jennings area. As the glaciers scraped across the land, they reshaped and scoured the earth. Approximately fourteen thousand years ago, when the last ice sheet started melting, water that was dammed up at Slippery Rock Creek formed glacial Lake Edmund. For centuries, sand, silt, and clay particles sifted down to the lake bottom before the ice disappeared and the lake drained away, leaving six inches of glacial till on top of the impervious soil below.

This soil set the stage for the prairie, which was further encouraged by a warm, dry period of weather seven thousand years ago. Such conditions persisted for three thousand years, allowing the Midwest prairie to extend into western Pennsylvania by 2000 B.C. Since then the weather has been colder and wetter, and most of western Pennsylvania has grown up into deciduous forest. But at Jennings the thin, glacial soil made it difficult for most trees to grow. With the additional help of prairie fires and browsing deer, elk, and bison, the prairie remnant was able to survive over the centuries.

When O. E. Jennings discovered the site, it was overgrown with trees and shrubs, but it also still supported several species of wildflowers more common on the midwestern prairies, including the blazing star *(Liatris spicata)*. This flower is found at only eight other nearby sites in western Pennsylvania, making it a rare wildflower in this portion of our state. However, this same flower is called gay feather in the Midwest, where it is a common species of

Blazing star, Jennings Environmental Education Center

the prairie. At Jennings its magenta-colored, composite flowers bloom on stems four to six feet high in late July and early August, forming what one naturalist called "an unforgettable purple haze."

In addition, other prairie wildflowers—such as boneset, which is considered an indicator of true prairie in the Midwest, and whorled rosinweed, also more characteristic of prairies and Midwest meadowlands—grow amid the blazing stars. In fact, the wildflower enthusiast can find a medley of lovely wildflowers blooming here in midsummer; Culver's root, or white wood candle, wild sweet william, tall meadow rue, ironweed, purple milkwort, and blue skullcap are just a few examples. There are also many species of tall sunflowers and coneflowers—yellow composites that have still not been completely sorted out according to species.

It is necessary to burn a quadrant of the area each spring to maintain the remnant prairie and thus to preserve its unique wildflowers as well as a relationship among three wild creatures—the meadow vole, the white crayfish, and the rare and endangered (in Pennsylvania) eastern massasauga rattlesnake. Take the Massasauga, Blazing Star, and Prairie Loop trails at Jennings to look for the small holes in the ground that are dug by the dryland white crayfish. The crayfish are often joined in their holes by shy, eighteen-inch-long massasauga rattlesnakes seeking shelter from the hot sun. The snakes are also looking for their prey, meadow voles, which in turn eat white crayfish. So the snakes, in effect, protect the white crayfish from their principal enemies. This symbiotic relationship between crayfish and rattlesnakes is being studied by naturalists working at Jennings. But while you can see the wildflowers and crayfish holes, the chances of spotting crayfishes, rattlesnakes, or meadow voles are slight.

The visitors center is open from 8:00 A.M. to 4:00 P.M. Monday through Friday and on weekend afternoons and evenings whenever special programs are offered. Here you can pick up a trail map, talk to knowledgeable personnel, and learn what there is to see at Jennings. Better yet, prepare ahead for your trip and write or call the Jennings Environmental Education Center, R.D. 1, Slippery Rock, PA 16057 (412-794-6011) and ask for a copy of the free schedule-of-events brochure.

The best time to see the prairie wildflowers in bloom is late July or early August. During two weekends, park naturalists lead free, one-and-a-half-hour walks through the prairie ecosystem at the height of the blazing star display. Wear light clothes and a sun hat, though, because it can be very warm on the open prairie.

If you want to explore other trails, go in the morning and take along a lunch to eat at one of the picnic tables. Then hike Ridge Trail (on the same side of the road as the visitors center), which is where one of the glaciers ended its advance over the land. The geological term for the mass of boulders and finer material it left behind is "terminal morraine."

We have visited Jennings twice to see the prairie bloom. The first time we explored the trails on our own and thoroughly enjoyed ourselves. The second time we joined a guided walk and not only enjoyed ourselves but learned a great deal. Jennings Environmental Education Center is an excellent place to go for a family outing, but it also encourages groups to visit. Just call the center to make a reservation.

To see a prairie in Pennsylvania is a unique experience. Even in the Midwest, there is no prairie remnant that looks quite like the Jennings relict, surrounded, as it is, by deciduous forest.

From Pittsburgh: Follow Interstate 79 for 40 miles north. Exit onto U.S. 422. Proceed east on 422 for 5.6 miles to the exit ramp for Pa. 528. Turn left. Follow 528 north 7.4 miles to the parking lots on either side of the road at the center.

50 WOLF CREEK NARROWS NATURAL AREA

Wolf Creek Narrows Natural Area, two miles northwest of Slippery Rock in Butler County, was purchased by the Western Pennsylvania Conservancy in 1979. The 125-acre tract is justly renowned for approximately ninety species of spring wildflowers, five rare plants—the showy orchis, spotted coralroot, and the bulblet, fragile, and walking ferns—and the narrow gorge with steep cliffs through which Wolf Creek flows. In addition, the forested hillsides bordering the creek have been undisturbed for eighty years, and some of the trees, which include stands of wild black cherry, yellow birch, American beech, sugar maple, red oak, tulip tree, and hemlock, are virgin timber.

The short (1.5 miles) but spectacularly beautiful Narrows Trail on the east side of Wolf Creek allows visitors to see the wide variety of native plants the area supports. Because the land had been in the same family since the Revolutionary War, it has been scrupulously cared for. Only in 1983 did the Conservancy complete its purchase with the flat, fifteen-acre piece that leads from the road into the narrows. This floodplain supports such wildflowers as skunk cabbage, marsh marigold, bluets, Canada and turk's-cap lilies, and mertensia.

Once you get into the narrows, the woods close in, and along the banks of Wolf Creek huge hemlock trees look much the same as they did to the first settlers who arrived in this part of Pennsylvania. Wood ducks and great blue herons can often be seen in this vicinity as well. But it is, as usual, the wildflowers that steal most of a hiker's attention. Trailing arbutus and wood anemones, trout lilies and cut-leaved toothworts, spring beauties and sharp-leaved hepaticas, large-flowered, snowy, and red trilliums, celandines, blood-root, Dutchman's-breeches, and squirrel corn—the litany could go on almost indefinitely.

No fewer than eleven species of violets, including the long-spurred and dog

Along Wolf Creek, Wolf Creek Narrows Natural Area

"stemless" violets, the arrow-leaved violet, and the smooth yellow (or Pennsylvania) violet, grow in the woods. In the spring you can also find the broad, smooth, onion-scented leaves of the wild leeks, or ramps, famous for their strongly scented bulbs, which mountain people in West Virginia dig up to eat at their early-spring ramp festivals. Only after the leaves wither, in June and July, do the flowers bloom. This is also the time to look for spotted coralroot, a rare orchid that lacks green pigment and bears its dull purple flowers with red-spotted, white-lobed tips on a leafless stalk.

Two of the rare ferns are best seen in summer. Then the streamerlike fronds of bulblet ferns hang in large masses over the limestone cliffs, rocky slopes, and steep banks of Wolf Creek Narrows, along with the little, evergreen walking fern, so-named because its long, narrow, finely tapered leaves touch the ground at their tips and sprout new plants. The fragile, or brittle, ferns appear in early spring in rock crevices but often disappear during summer droughts.

Probably the loveliest of the rare plants at Wolf Creek Narrows is the showy orchis, which appears on Pennsylvania's Vulnerable Plant Species List. With its cluster of four rose-hooded, white-lipped flowers and its two wide, green leaves, this spring-blooming orchid is quite a prize to discover. The smallest and earliest species of trillium, the snow, or dwarf white, trillium, is also a vulnerable plant in Pennsylvania and is growing at Wolf Creek Narrows only because Conservancy members rescued plants from a construction project in the southern part of the state and transplanted them. They are not growing in an ideal environment, since they prefer a more southern clime; although alive, they are not thriving.

However, in the case of the showy orchis, which *is* growing in its natural environment, it is vulnerable precisely because people have dug up so many and attempted to transplant them into their own gardens. Such meddling is nearly always disastrous to wild plants, particularly wild orchids. That is why the Western Pennsylvania Conservancy has purchased the land—to protect it from development and plant-stealers—as well as to encourage people to hike over the trails and appreciate wildflowers on their own turf.

Spring and early summer are the best seasons to visit. There are no facilities other than the trail, so bring along a snack and water, binoculars, a hand lens, and good wildflower, tree, and fern guides. Since the trail is short and relatively easy, families, garden clubs, and nature societies would all enjoy an outing here, especially if a wild-plant expert comes along.

From Pittsburgh: Take Interstate 79 north approximately 45 miles to Route 108. Follow 108 east into Slippery Rock. Turn left at the light in the center of town (258 north) and go one block. Then turn left onto West Water Street. Drive 1.7 miles until you reach the iron bridge over Wolf Creek. Cross the bridge and continue partway up the hill to the first left, where you turn onto an old farm lane. Pull off and park along (but not on) the lane. To start the trail, walk back across the bridge and turn left onto Narrows Trail, paralleling the stream.

51 COOK FOREST STATE PARK

Cook Forest State Park, on the northwestern Allegheny Plateau, was the locale for *Unconquered,* the Cecil B. deMille movie about the siege of Fort Pitt, featuring Gary Cooper, Paulette Goddard, and Boris Karloff. The park was chosen, according to James A. Kell, then secretary of the State Department of Forests and Waters, because it had "the largest remaining stand of virgin pine and hemlock in the East," and therefore "appeared as the most likely of the

Clarion River Lookout, Cook Forest State Park

many areas suggested to still retain natural areas and conditions as they existed about the middle of the 18th century."

Cook Forest State Park has not changed much in the forty years since the film was made. Many of the same trails—Hemlock, Rhododendron, Deer Park, Joyce Kilmer, Mohawk, Seneca—still exist, and, except for damage from two severe hurricanes and one flood, the same virgin trees have merely put on forty more growth rings.

There are three areas of virgin timber in the park, two of which are easily accessible by foot. In addition, you can canoe in the Clarion River, drive up to Seneca Point for a fine view, take the lovely Nature Trail (built by the Civilian Conservation Corps), visit the small nature museum, or shop at the excellent regional crafts center.

To reach the Forest Cathedral area, which contains a hundred acres of virgin pine as well as a sprinkling of sweet birch, black cherry, red maple, red oak, yellow birch, and cucumber trees, park at the park office lot, pick up a brochure, and walk past the children's fishing pond, across the bridge, and along the road leading through the park cabin area, where Rhododendron

Trail begins. The trail parallels Tom's Run for a short way beyond a swinging bridge on your left before beginning a gentle climb through a lovely hemlock–white pine forest.

At the intersection of Rhododendron and Indian trails, turn left on Indian Trail. You will immediately notice the giant white pines, some of which are more than three hundred years old. Many are three to four feet in diameter and close to two hundred feet tall. These pines are called cork pine because of their thick, corklike bark. The understory of moss and ferns is typical of an area of dense shade, although extensive browsing by deer also keeps it in trim. Down near Tom's Run, where it is wetter, enormous one-hundred-year-old rhododendron shrubs grow.

When you reach Longfellow Trail, turn left again. Short trails identified by letters (A, B, C, D, and E) crisscross back and forth through the heart of the Cathedral, a Registered National Natural Landmark. If you have had enough walking, follow Longfellow Trail back to Birch Trail. Turn left on Birch Trail, a flat, easy trail that parallels the park road back to the office. This is approximately a three-mile circuit.

To see the second virgin-timber area, instead of turning left on Birch Trail, cross the park road to Hemlock Trail and follow it uphill until it becomes Deer Park Trail. This aptly named trail runs through an open, hurricane-damaged area where the deer are both abundant and bold. As you walk along the trail, you can hear and sometimes see a woods road off to your right, with a steady stream of traffic heading for Seneca Point Lookout and a fire tower. Driving is the easy way to get there. However, you will miss one of the park's nicest trails, Seneca Trail, which intersects Deer Park Trail. Turn right up to Seneca Point, passing through a long rock fissure and a fine rhododendron stand before reaching both the fire tower and the lookout, the latter a huge outcrop of boulders overlooking the Clarion River.

Retrace your steps along Seneca Trail straight down the mountainside, where you will walk through seventy acres of virgin hemlock. The last part of this trail is narrow and slippery in places, but it is easier to descend than to ascend. The park office is at its base, so pick up your car and drive along the park road until you reach the Log Cabin Historical and Nature Center on the right, with its small display of lumbering tools and nature-related items. The Longfellow Trail up to the Forest Cathedral also begins here and is the fastest, easiest way to see that area.

From here proceed to the Sawmill Craft Center, where local crafts are for sale as well as tickets for a variety of summer events in the adjacent theater. Craft workshops are also offered on a weekly basis.

Behind the craft center the level, circular 1.5-mile Nature Trail leads through a woods of younger, but still lovely, hardwood and hemlock trees.

Here are large American beeches, which, in late summer and early autumn, support a huge colony of the parasitic wildflower beechdrop. Pileated woodpeckers, hermit thrushes, white-throated sparrows, eastern chipmunks, and both gray and red squirrels were the wild creatures we saw during a visit in late September. This area also has a car entrance and parking for the handicapped, so they can enjoy the smaller, paved trail through the same lovely woods.

With twenty-seven miles of foot trails, two bridle trails, several picnic areas, family camping, fishing in the Clarion River, and a swimming pool, there is plenty to do at Cook Forest State Park. Even in the winter you can cross-country ski, snowmobile, skate, and sled at designated areas.

From Interstate 80: Follow Interstate 80 west to Brookville, Exit 13. Then take Pa. Route 36 north 15.3 miles until it crosses the Clarion River and enters the park.

52 ERIE NATIONAL WILDLIFE REFUGE

Ducks and beavers are the main attractions at Erie National Wildlife Refuge, in Crawford County in the northwestern part of the state. From April until November ducks can be observed on the numerous ponds and marshy areas. Early morning and evening are the best times to glimpse beavers at work.

Other bird species abundant at the refuge include nesting warblers like the common yellowthroat, mourning, blue-winged, magnolia, hooded, yellow, and Blackburnian. Among the thirteen species of sparrows you could see here, Henslow's sparrow is the rarest. If you're interested in birds of prey, you can scan the skies for Cooper's, red-shouldered, and sharp-skinned hawks or spend your evenings in search of great-horned, barred, and screech owls.

Along Tsuga Nature Trail behind the refuge office, a succession of spring wildflowers, such as painted, purple, and white trilliums, hepaticas, dwarf ginsengs, trout lilies, spring beauties, and marsh marigolds, can be seen. In addition, you may see the resident woodchuck, numerous painted turtles basking on logs in the beaver pond, or such nesting duck species as black ducks, blue-winged teal, and the most spectacular North American duck of all—the wood duck.

A second, shorter trail, Beaver Run, can be reached by driving down the refuge's entrance road and turning left on Route 198 for .3 mile, then right onto the gravel Cemetery Road. Proceed .3 mile; after another .3 mile on a blacktop road, turn right on Hanks Road and drive a further mile. The parking lot on the left is for hikers. Beaver Run Trail consists of two half-mile seg-

Canada goose in marsh, Erie National Wildlife Refuge

ments. Along the first part you will pass a pond. The second section leads around a cornfield, a good place to watch deer feeding in the evening.

Erie National Wildlife Refuge is the only national wildlife refuge in Pennsylvania. Unlike most national wildlife refuges, Erie does not have a designated auto-tour, because the numerous gravel roads that wind through the 7,994-acre refuge are owned by the townships. However, once you have visited the refuge headquarters and hiked the 1.6-mile Tsuga Nature Trail and the Beaver Run Trail, you can drive slowly through the refuge on well-marked roads, stopping frequently to scan the numerous marshy and brushy areas for wild turkeys, ducks, and songbirds.

At .4 mile east of the refuge office's entrance road, turn right onto a gravel road (McFadden); .8 mile further on scan the pond on the right for ducks. Drive another .3 mile, turn right on Shaffer Road, and after .5 mile turn left on New Road. There is a beaver pond .2 mile further along on the left side of the road, but instead of beaver you may see great blue herons fishing.

Another 1.4 mile brings you to State Highway 27. Turn right on Boland Road and drive .4 mile until you reach Richie Road, where you turn left. After .7 mile there is a marsh on the left where wood ducks nest. Bushes beside the road are filled with songbirds like yellow warblers and song sparrows in late April. A parking lot on the right, .4 mile beyond the marsh, can be used while you stretch your legs, walk along the pond to the left of the road, and scan the smaller ponds to the right for water birds.

Return to your car and drive another .5 mile until you reach a larger, lily pad–covered pond on the right. A parking lot allows you to leave your car and take a short path through a wooded area to an observation blind. The blind looks out over Reitz Pond, where you can observe Canada geese, wood ducks in nesting boxes, and great blue herons.

This wetland area continues .2 mile until the road intersects State Route 173, where you turn right and continue for .8 mile. Make a right onto the blacktop road and drive for .1 mile. Then make a second right onto the gravel Vincent Road for 1.4 miles until you reach the Deer Run Overlook. Here you can enjoy a scenic view of the valley below and the largest impoundment on the refuge (135 acres). Bald eagles and hawks are frequently spotted in this valley.

When you leave the parking area, make a right, continue .7 mile, then make another right and drive for .4 mile. Here Oil Creek Road makes a T with Route 27, where you can either go west to Meadville or east to Titusville.

Erie National Wildlife Refuge has no picnic areas or campgrounds, but it is possible to arrange for group tours ahead of time. Just write to the Refuge Manager, R.D. 1, Guys Mills, PA 16327, or call 814-789-3585. There are plans to build a fishing pier for handicapped people at the Richie Road pond and to renovate some historical buildings on the property.

Although spring and fall are the best times to see the vast numbers of migrating and nesting waterfowl and songbirds, two cross-country ski trails have made the refuge a popular place in the winter for people in nearby Meadville and Erie. One trail is only a mile; the other is a three-mile loop through woods and open fields, where white-tailed deer and wild turkeys can sometimes be seen. This trail has recently been opened for hiking as well and is now called the Deer Run Trail.

Erie National Wildlife Refuge was created in 1959 to provide nesting, feeding, and resting habitat for ducks and geese. The land was purchased with funds provided from the sale of Migratory Bird Hunting and Conservation Stamps. Much of the land near the pools is cultivated and produces such crops as winter wheat, buckwheat, corn, oats, and a grass/legume mixture to supplement the natural food found here.

From Erie: Take Interstate 79 for 28 miles south to Exit 37, Pa. 198. Follow 198 east approximately 17 miles to Guys Mills. Continue on Pa. 198 for .7 mile to refuge office entrance.

53 PYMATUNING LAKE

Pymatuning Lake, on the Ohio-Pennsylvania border in northwestern Crawford County, is six miles long with seventy miles of shoreline. Before this area was dammed to conserve water and control flooding in the Shenango and Ohio River valleys, it was an inaccessible, wooded bog—a paradise to the few naturalists who explored it, but impenetrable to most other people.

Ornithologist George Miksch Sutton was sent by W. E. Todd of the Carnegie Museum in Pittsburgh to explore Pymatuning Swamp during the 1920s. Todd, who knew the area was to be dammed, wanted a record of the wildlife of the swamp before it became a lake. Sutton discovered "a 25 mile area of boggy lakes, cattail marshes, tamaracks, hemlocks, pitcher plants, royal ferns, lady's slippers, sundew and poison sumac, an untamed wilderness where the drama of wild-life goes on uninterrupted."

Then it had 134 nesting bird species and 74 migrant species, but because there was little in the way of marshlands and no open water, waterfowl like American coots, Canada geese, gadwalls, and greater and lesser yellowlegs were migrants rather than summer residents, and bald eagles were only occasional visitors.

All that changed when the dam was constructed in 1933 and the Game Commission began creating a wildlife refuge where migrating waterfowl could feed and rest. Huge fields of corn, buckwheat, and rye were planted to tempt Canada geese to land. The new refuge also attracted American coots, gadwalls, mallards, black ducks, wood ducks, blue-winged teal, and both species of yellowlegs, some of which stayed to breed. Best of all, three years after the lake was impounded, bald eagles started nesting in the wildlife refuge. By 1986 Pymatuning had five nesting pairs and between thirteen and seventeen adult eagles in the area.

Today the eagles are the main attraction for visitors at the Game Commission's Waterfowl Museum on Ford Island. From the porch of the museum, visitors can watch bald eagles flying over the lake and fishing, or, if it is April or May, nesting on a small island a quarter of a mile away. A spotting scope provides a close-up view, but the actual distance is far enough that the birds are not bothered.

Area 7 marsh, Pymatuning Lake

The museum was erected in 1938 to display 410 mounted specimens of all the waterfowl and bird-of-prey species found at Pymatuning, as well as family bird groupings and numerous furbearing animals of the region. It should be the first stop for visitors because time spent studying the beautifully mounted birds will help later when exploring the trails, marshes, and lakeshore. (You can also find out from the museum manager which dirt roads are open to the public.)

Parking and admission to the museum are free, and the museum is open from March 1 until November 30 from 8:00 A.M. to 4:00 P.M. Monday through Friday and from 10:00 A.M. to 6:00 P.M. on weekends. The hours are subject to change, however, so it is best to call the museum manager (814-683-5545) before you visit. Tours of the museum and wildlife films for groups can also be arranged in advance. Outside the museum a quarter-mile nature trail along the lake features two overlooks of the lake and forty labeled shrubs.

From the museum drive southwest past a fish-feeding area below the spillway. Legislative Route 20006 then bears due south for two-tenths of a mile until it gradually veers southeast and crosses Pa. 285. Turn right toward the town of Espyville, two miles away. If you want to see what the Ohio side of Pymatuning looks like, drive across the Andover-Espyville Causeway. On a windy day, waves slam against the side of the causeway, and diving ducks can often be seen in the water below. During migration large flocks of tundra (formerly whistling) swans land on the lake.

Return on Pa. 285 until it once again intersects with Legislative Route 20006. This time turn right toward Hartstown. Since many of the wetland areas at Pymatuning are closed to casual visitors, the best place to see migrant and nesting waterfowl is outside Hartstown off Route 322, which crosses Pa. 18 at the edge of town. Cross an overhead bridge east of town, turn right and go down under the bridge, then follow a graveled road north along the Bessemer Railroad tracks. This parallels an excellent marsh area (called Area 7 on Game Commission maps).

We explored Area 7 one April with members of our local Juniata Valley Audubon Society and, despite frequent rainstorms, saw many mallards, buffleheads, American coots, blue-winged teal, gadwalls, ring-necked ducks, and American shovelers in the water. Ring-billed gulls, purple martins, and tree swallows could be seen swooping over the marsh, and once we spotted a great blue heron almost perfectly camouflaged among brushy growth on the far shore.

Later we drove past huge planted fields where we could see Canada geese wherever we looked. Goose management is a major concern of the Game Commission. Pymatuning has a nesting and summering population of 3,000 geese, with 15,000 geese stopping over at the peak of fall migration. A wintering population of 3,000 geese also stays in the area, so Canada geese can be seen wandering across the dirt roads and over the fields year-round. In between the fields we saw small sloughs containing hooded mergansers, greater scaup, and lesser yellowlegs, while the occasional patches of woods were blanketed with the dainty blossoms of spring beauty.

Along the southern arm of the lake, north of Jamestown, Pennsylvania, is Pymatuning State Park, with 832 family-camping units in four areas. Every conceivable outdoor activity seems possible at the park, including cross-country skiing, snowmobiling, and ice skating in winter, boating and swimming in summer, and hiking year-round.

Every season has its attractions at Pymatuning Lake, but if you are primarily interested in watching the incredible array of birds attracted to the lake during migration, April, May, and September are the best months to visit. To view the nesting bald eagles, April is the ideal time.

From Erie: Take Interstate 79 south approximately 30 miles to Exit 36. Proceed west on U.S. 6–322 to Conneaut Lake. Continue northwest onto U.S. 6 until you reach Linesville. At the center of the town turn south (left) onto Legislative Route 20006, which leads to the Waterfowl Museum (about one mile from the town on your left).

54 ALLEGHENY NATIONAL FOREST

The Allegheny National Forest sprawls over most of four northwestern counties—McKean, Forest, Elk, and Warren. It is, as national forests throughout the United States are described, a "land of many uses," where gas wells intrude in scenic areas and "managed" forests border on natural areas left forever wild. Snowmobile and trail-bike trails are provided for the motorist, while many miles of hiking trails are maintained for those who prefer foot-power.

Campers could spend weeks exploring here, but for those who have only a day to spare, three outstanding places to see are Heart's Content Scenic Area, Tidioute Overlook, and the Hickory Creek Wilderness Area. The latter is the only national wilderness area within a five-state radius.

To begin the day, stop at Tidioute Overlook and take the two short paths that lead to separate overlooks of the Allegheny River—one upstream and the other downstream. From here continue to Heart's Content Scenic Area.

This outstanding 121-acre tract of virgin white pines, hemlocks, and American beeches was declared a Registered Natural Landmark in 1977. A mile-long, self-guided trail over almost level ground meanders past many giants, giving visitors a glimpse of what a white pine–hemlock–northern hardwoods forest looked like before the loggers moved in. Birds flit so high in the coniferous canopy that it is difficult to see them, but their songs are the only sounds you hear as you walk on a carpet of evergreen needles.

Halfway along the trail are a memorial to the logging firm Wheeler and Dusenberry, which donated the first twenty acres of this forest to the government in 1922, and several springs that mark the source of the west branch of Tionesta Creek. At this point the trail crosses the brook and heads upstream (west) through a mixed conifer-hardwood forest that includes red maple, black cherry, white ash, and yellow and black birches as well as the more magnificent American beeches.

Finally, near the end of the trail, a hand-hewn white pine is displayed in an open shelter. Accompanying photographs illustrate how a tree trunk becomes a beam. As soon as you cross the border of the scenic area, there is a pleasant picnic ground, where you can lunch before heading off to explore a portion of the Hickory Creek Wilderness Area.

Heart's Content Natural Area, Allegheny National Forest

From the picnic ground, cross the road and take the short trail through a red pine plantation—a cool, dense retreat on a hot summer day—that leads directly to the Hickory Creek Wilderness Area along the orange-blazed, eleven-mile-loop Hickory Creek Trail. This is a popular backpacking trail, and most people make the gently rolling hike in two days. But for a relatively short and easy afternoon hike, follow the trail for a little over half a mile through an open woods, where beds of spring beauties and violets bloom in mid-April. When you reach a fork, turn left and, watching carefully for blazes, proceed through a large, second-growth beech–hemlock forest, where veeries and solitary vireos sing.

Make certain you cross a woods road a short way along the left fork, and then look for a spring to the right. Less than half a mile from the spring, you will come to a tributary stream and the remnants of an old bridge to your right. Ford the stream on stepping stones and immediately ascend the trail, which will then overlook the stream below. In this area is at least one eight-trunked red oak, seemingly an unusual phenomenon except that a seventrunked one grows in the hemlock forest and several six-trunked ones can also be seen along the trail.

By the time you reach an obvious blowdown area, you have walked more than two miles. Since you must retrace your steps to the parking lot, this is a good place to turn around. Once you return to your car, you can take a quicker return back to Erie by driving the 3.8 miles to the paved road and then turning right rather than left onto the paved road. Follow it north 11.5 miles to Warren, where you can pick up Route 6 west toward Erie.

Note: The great May 1985 tornado leveled eight hundred acres of timber in the justifiably famous Tionesta Scenic Area, also in the Allegheny National Forest. All but five hundred feet of the one-mile interpretive trail was destroyed. According to a letter I received from Nancy Schuler, information technician for the Allegheny National Forest, in April 1986, plans are to build a new loop trail northwest of the old one. It will be approximately 7,700 feet long, with a 1,900-foot loop. Plans call for it to go through different sizes and species of trees, cross four footbridges, and pass twenty-five to thirty interpretive points. By the time this book is published, the trail should be completed, but write ahead to the Office of Information, Allegheny National Forest, Box 847, Warren, PA 16365, to make sure. To reach this area from Warren, follow U.S. 6 east to Ludlow about fifteen miles. Take a right turn onto Forest Road (FR) 133. (Watch for signs.) Then look for a right turn on FR 133E. (Again, there should be a sign.) Park on widened portions of the road shoulder.

From Erie to Heart's Content: Follow Route 19 south 10 miles to Waterford. In Waterford turn left (east) on Route 97; drive 8 miles to Union City. Turn left on Route 6 and drive 37 miles to Youngsville. Three miles beyond Youngsville take the exit for Route 62 south. Drive 15.7 miles (.1 mile beyond the bridge that turns right across the river to Tidioute) and turn left. Drive 1.3 miles and turn left into the Tidioute Overlook. From here continue 8.9 miles to a gravel forest road, where you turn right. Continue for 3.6 miles to Heart's Content (on your left).

55 PRESQUE ISLE STATE PARK

Presque Isle State Park in northwestern Pennsylvania encompasses the pork chop–shaped peninsula jutting into Lake Erie directly across Presque Isle Bay from the city of Erie. Naturalists know the peninsula for two things—its unique plant life and the incredible number of birds that stop over during their spring and fall migrations.

Open surf on Lake Erie, Presque Isle State Park

Presque Isle means "almost an island" in French. The peninsula was created more than a thousand years ago when the action of westerly winds, water currents, and waves on glacial sand caused a recurving sandspit to form. Weather conditions continue to exert their influence on the peninsula, changing its shape from year to year and its location from decade to decade. In fact, during the last hundred years, Presque Isle has moved almost a half mile east.

These changes are graphically illustrated by maps at the park's excellent Nature Center. The first building on the left side of Peninsula Drive, nine-tenths of a mile from the park entrance, the center is open from Memorial Day until Labor Day.

The Nature Center was created in what was formerly an administration and first-aid building by the combined efforts of the Presque Isle Audubon Society, the Northwestern Pennsylvania Duck Hunters' Association, and the Department of Environmental Resources. Its focal point is a series of illustrated panels accompanied by a text that explains the plant succession of Presque Isle. Beginning with a photograph of the "litter zone," which illustrates the problems caused by human overuse of the 3,200-acre peninsula, the panels also explain Presque Isle's six ecological zones: the water's edge, the sand plain, the dunes and ridges, the old lagoons and marshes, the thicket subclimax forests, and the climax forests. Other displays include the butterflies of Presque Isle, mounted ducks, a children's touch-and-see section, and a unique mobile of natural objects. Movies, lectures, and naturalist-led walks are also scheduled frequently during the season.

Once you are acquainted with what the peninsula has to offer, there are two major undeveloped areas to explore—the Ecological Reservation and Gull Point Sanctuary. Continue following Peninsula Drive until it bears right and becomes Marina Drive and then East Fisher Road. East Fisher Road curves left and is then called Thompson Drive. Thompson Drive follows around Misery Bay and finally makes a left turn up to the north end of the peninsula and the open waters of Lake Erie. Park at Budny Beach, leave any pets in the car, and walk to the end of the parking lot to an area prominently marked Bird Sanctuary.

The piping plover, which is now on the federal endangered list, once nested at Presque Isle, as did the common tern. The Bureau of State Parks, with the help of the Pennsylvania Game Commission, is making an effort to encourage the return of these birds by closing off suitable nesting areas in the sanctuary with posts and plainly marked signs, so please be careful when you quietly walk to Gull Point.

The species of water birds to be seen along the Lake Erie beach and in the lagoons, which constantly change their configurations from year to year, are similar to those found at the Atlantic seashore. During migration, birders are out in the area in all kinds of weather, hoping to spot birds like the Arctic tern and the chuck-will's-widow, species rarely seen in Pennsylvania. However, they're more likely to see the more common sora, least bittern, black-bellied plover, dunlin, red-breasted merganser, and common loon.

Botanists also are intrigued by Presque Isle. Here they can find beach pea, lupine, wormwood, and lyre-leaved rock cress on the moving sand plain. Two prairie grasses—switchgrass and little blue-stem—are found in Pennsylvania only on Presque Isle's sand plain. Other species that are found in Pennsylvania only on the peninsula are silverweed, burreed, variegated horsetail, and white-stem pondweed. None of these plants is rare farther north, but they do reach their southernmost limit on Presque Isle. In fact, fifty-five of the Pennsylvania Species of Special Concern have been found on the peninsula, including the endangered Kalm's lobelia.

After thoroughly exploring the sanctuary, return to your car and continue on Pine Tree Road until you reach a sign on the left for the Ecological Reservation. Park and study the map on the board showing the myriad of trails you can take through the thicket subclimax and climax forest of Presque Isle's interior. The paved Sidewalk Trail cuts directly across the peninsula and is a good place to view a variety of songbirds. It also makes walking very easy even during a downpour.

You may be tempted to spend an entire day exploring the Ecological Reservation since the paths are varied and frequently skirt inland ponds and marshes. Occasionally you may spot an osprey perched in a tree beside a pond or a great blue heron stalking through the marshes. During migration this area is filled with dozens of songbird species as well. Muskrats, white-tailed deer, and eastern chipmunks are also common.

Presque Isle has been named one of the ten birding hot spots in the nation during migration. The best time of the birding year usually occurs in mid-May, especially when the weather is bad. If the birds cannot cross Lake Erie, they pile up on the peninsula, and then a true paradise for birders occurs. On such a weekend we identified one hundred species of birds—including a Hudsonian godwit, a short-billed dowitcher, and a dunlin—in the vicinity of the sanctuary and in the open water of Lake Erie just offshore.

The Ecological Reservation, on the other hand, was filled with songbirds. We identified eighteen species of warblers, and for once it was easy to see these flitting, restless birds since each tree held dozens of them. But we made our best sighting in the pouring rain as we walked along Sidewalk Trail. A rare sedge wren popped up from the base of a shrub and paused long enough for us to see its buffy undertail coverts and streaked crown before it flew back down in the underbrush and disappeared.

Botanists will enjoy searching for emerging plants in spring, when there are no crowds at Presque Isle. But late July and August are the best times to see the beautiful rose gentian, purple gerardia, and yellow flax in bloom, as well as rare plants like the Kalm's lobelia.

Presque Isle has had as many as five million visitors in one year. If you choose to visit Presque Isle as a naturalist in the summer, it might be wise to imitate members of the Presque Isle Audubon Society, who arrive at dawn and leave by 10:00 A.M., just as the hordes of recreationists arrive. However, the chance to swim in the surf of Lake Erie will be as close as a Pennsylvanian can get to ocean swimming without leaving the state. Boating is also allowed, and the East Boat Livery rents canoes, rowboats, and motorboats. Since the park is open throughout the winter, ice skating and ice fishing are also allowed. A winter-sports concession, located at the Water Works Pavilion No. 2, is open from November 1 to March 31.

Presque Isle, with its possible 318 species of birds and more than 500 species of flowering plants and ferns, can keep any naturalist busy for a lifetime.

From Erie: Take West 12th Street west until it intersects with Route 832 (Penin-

sula Drive). Turn right and proceed directly onto the peninsula. Visitors from out of town should come to Erie via Interstate 79 and exit at 26th Street. Turn left and drive approximately one mile until 26th Street intersects with Route 832. Turn right and continue to the peninsula.

SELECTED
BIBLIOGRAPHY

Aron, Jean. *The Short Hiker: The Unicorn Hunter's Guide to Gentle Trails in Central Penn's Woods.* 1982. (Revised 1987.)

Berkeley, Edmund, and Dorothy Smith Berkeley. *The Life and Travels of John Bartram: From Lake Ontario to the River St. John.* Tallahassee: University Presses of Florida, 1982.

Brett, James J. *Feathers in the Wind: The Mountain and the Migration.* Kempton, Pa.: Hawk Mountain Sanctuary Association, 1973.

Broun, Maurice. *Hawks Aloft: The Story of Hawk Mountain.* New York: Dodd, Mead and Co., 1948.

Cruickshank, Helen Gere, ed. *John and William Bartram's America.* New York: Doubleday and Co., 1961.

Durant, Mary, and Michael Harwood. *On the Road with John James Audubon.* New York: Dodd, Mead and Co., 1980.

Erdman, Dr. Kimball S., and Paul G. Weigman. *Preliminary List of Natural Areas in Pennsylvania.* Pittsburgh: Western Pennsylvania Conservancy, 1974.

Geyer, Alan R., and William H. Bolles. *Outstanding Scenic Geological Features of Pennsylvania.* Harrisburg: Bureau of Topographic and Geologic Survey, 1979.

Giza, Eugene V., and Gayle Giza. *Presque Isle: A Place for All Seasons.* 1985.

Heintzelman, Donald S. *A Guide to Hawk Watching in North America.* University Park: The Pennsylvania State University Press, 1979.

Hoffman, Carolyn. *Fifty Hikes in Eastern Pennsylvania: Day Hikes and Backpacks from the Susquehanna to the Poconos.* Woodstock, Vt.: Backcountry Publications, 1982.

Hoffmann, Donald. *Frank Lloyd Wright's Fallingwater: The House and Its History.* New York: Dover Publications, 1978.

Lawrence, Susannah, and Barbara Gross. *The Audubon Society Field Guide to the Natural Places of the Mid-Atlantic States: Inland.* New York: Pantheon Books, 1984.

Niering, William A. *The Life of the Marsh.* New York: McGraw-Hill, 1966.

Pennsylvania Hiking Trails in State Parks, Game Lands and Elsewhere. Keystone Trails Association, 1981. (10th edition due out in 1987).

The Pennsylvania Naturalist. State College, Pa.: Shafer Publishing Co. Vol. 1 (1978) to Vol. 3 (1981).

Randour, Bill, and Alan Van Dine, eds. *Fifty Years of the Western Pennsylvania Conservancy.* Pittsburgh: Western Pennsylvania Conservancy, 1982.

Stull, Jean, James A. Stull, and Gerald M. McWilliams. *Birds of Erie County Pennsylvania Including Presque Isle.* Elgin, Pa.: Allegheny Press, 1985.

Sundquist, Bruce, and Clifford C. Ham, eds. *Hiking Guide to Western Pennsylvania.* Pittsburgh: Pittsburgh Council American Youth Hostels, 1986.

Sutton, George Miksch. "The Birds of Pymatuning Swamp and Conneaut Lake, Crawford County, Pennsylvania." *Annals of the Carnegie Museum* 18 (1927–28): 19–239.

Thwaites, Tom. *Fifty Hikes in Central Pennsylvania.* Woodstock, Vt.: Backcountry Publications, 1985.

————. *Fifty Hikes in Western Pennsylvania: Walks and Day Hikes from the Laurel Highlands to Lake Erie.* Woodstock, Vt.: Backcountry Publications, 1983. (Revision due out in 1987.)

Tomorrow's Oasis Today: Proceedings of the Conference on Presque Isle and the Erie Bayfront (Sept. 26–27, 1985). Copies available from: Erie County Department of Planning, Erie County Court House, Room 13, Erie, PA 16501.

Wilshusen, J. Peter. *Geology of the Appalachian Trail in Pennsylvania.* Harrisburg: Pennsylvania Geological Survey, 1983.